MORE
EARLY AMERICAN STENCILS
IN COLOR

Stenciled Album spread, c. 1845, New York State. 80″ x 72″. This coverlet shows a boldness of overall design and individual motif that is most unusual in Early American stenciled fabrics. (America Hurrah Antiques, N.Y.C.)

MORE
EARLY AMERICAN STENCILS
IN COLOR

Taken from Fabric, Furniture, and Tin
Together with a Gallery of Stenciled Quilts and Coverlets
and
Full Instructions on How to Stencil

Alice Bancroft Fjelstul and Patricia Brown Schad
with
Barbara Marhoefer

E. P. DUTTON   NEW YORK

To our husbands and children:
Dean Fjelstul, Beth, Sarah, and Chip;
Robert Schad, Christina, Donald, and Cynthia;
Joe Marhoefer, John, Mary Beth, Melinda, and Laurie.

ACKNOWLEDGMENTS

Our special thanks go to the owners of the historic quilts and coverlets and other historic pieces illustrated in this book, which have been so generously shared with us. We are grateful to the museums for the use of their photographs, and especially to the individuals at the museums, who were so helpful and enthusiastic. Cyril I. Nelson, our editor at E. P. Dutton, has also been very helpful to us in this project.

We particularly wish to acknowledge the following persons who so kindly gave us help in our research: America Hurrah Antiques, New York City; Joanne Bondy, Minneapolis Public Library, Walker Branch; Nancy V. Bryk, Henry Ford Museum and Greenfield Village, Dearborn, Michigan; Shirley Spaulding DeVoe, Bridgewater, Connecticut; Richard C. Eustice, Strawbery Banke, Inc., Portsmouth, New Hampshire; Paul Flack, Furlong, Pennsylvania; Mary Grumbaum, Dallas, Texas; Bryce and Donna Hamilton, Minneapolis, Minnesota; Nancy Hannah, Minneapolis, Minnesota; Margot Strand Jensen, Aurora, Colorado; Mrs. Robert Keegan, Hudson, Ohio; Kelter-Malcé Antiques, New York City; Jane Kristiansson, Minneapolis Public Library, Walker Branch; Jeanne Leach, Plymouth, Minnesota; Mr. and Mrs. Foster McCarl, Jr.; Betty Nibbelink, Brockport, New York; Jane Nylander, Old Sturbridge Village, Sturbridge, Massachusetts; Patsy Orlofsky, South Salem, New York; Penny J. Sanders, Society for the Preservation of New England Antiquities, Boston, Massachusetts; Barbara Hunt Smith, Oak Bluffs, Massachusetts; Vivian Walvatne, Minneapolis, Minnesota; Marilyn Woodin, Kalona, Iowa.

CONTENTS

PREFACE   vii

Chapter One: THE STENCIL: SIMPLE TOOL, HUMBLE TOOL   1

Chapter Two: EARLY AMERICAN TREASURES: THE STENCILED QUILT AND COVERLET   6

Chapter Three: PATTERNS FROM EIGHT STENCILED QUILTS AND COVERLETS   19

Chapter Four: STENCILS FROM FURNITURE AND TIN; ALSO THE WORK OF ESTHER STEVENS BRAZER   64

Chapter Five: JANET WARING AND STENCILS FROM HER COLLECTION   89

Chapter Six: STENCILS FOR CHILDREN'S ROOMS   107

Chapter Seven: STENCILS FOR A COUNTRY KITCHEN FROM THE JANET WARING COLLECTION   116

Chapter Eight: THEOREMS   125

Chapter Nine: STEP-BY-STEP DIRECTIONS ON HOW TO STENCIL, TOGETHER WITH PATTERNS FROM AN EARLY AMERICAN CURTAIN, A VALANCE, AND A TABLECLOTH   129

NOTES   142

BIBLIOGRAPHY   143

Silk panel stamped "Mrs. L. L. Cole, P.O. Box 1114, Chicago. 19½″ x 18½″. This example of late stenciling was given a silver medal by the Illinois State Agricultural Society, which was inscribed "Awarded to / Mrs. L. L. Cole / For Cloth ornamented / with indelible Fluid / at the Fair of / 1866." (Collection of James and Judith Milne; photograph courtesy America Hurrah Antiques, N.Y.C.)

PREFACE

In our first book, *Early American Wall Stencils in Color*, we presented many authentic wall-stencil patterns, all of which were large, bold patterns. After publication of the book, those in our classes and lectures earnestly requested some smaller patterns, so we kept adding to our collections.

While researching the first book, we had uncovered a little-known collection of Early American stencils donated to the Society for the Preservation of New England Antiquities in Boston and to The Metropolitan Museum of Art in New York City by Janet Waring, a pioneer in stencil research who published *Early American Stencils on Walls and Furniture* in 1937.

We also became fascinated with Early American stenciled quilts and coverlets. We knew of only a half-dozen examples, so we started a thorough and energetic search for others. We eventually tracked down more than thirty stenciled pieces in museums and private collections.

Also, we reviewed our own collections of tin and furniture for engaging stencils. We brought together a special group of designs for use in decorating children's rooms and kitchens; this was in response to another frequent request from stencilers.

Meanwhile, we worked to perfect our methods of easy-to-do stenciling, looking for new and better materials with an eye to low cost.

This second book is the result of our continued research into Early American stenciling. We have found that since the Bicentennial in 1976, Americans from Florida to Seattle have become more and more interested in American folk arts. These enthusiasts have daily become more numerous, and they have also become our friends. Their interest encourages ours. Our thanks to one and all!

NOTE

All of the patterns presented in this book are authentic, and all of them were traced from the original stenciled pieces. The patterns are reproduced in full size unless otherwise noted. Many of the patterns are shown in the original colors; however, in chapters four through seven we stenciled many of the patterns in our own color combinations for the sake of variety.

Detail from Album spread, page ii.

Detail from Album spread, page ii.

Chapter One

THE STENCIL: SIMPLE TOOL, HUMBLE TOOL

After having spent a good deal of time studying wall stencils, we became aware that walls were not the only things stenciled long ago; many other types of stenciling were popular.

At antiques shows we were soon able to find other types of stenciling: on tin boxes, crocks, trays, furniture, and wooden butter boxes. Among our first discoveries were two delightful trays—one with a profusion of pheasants and leaves, the other with a charming girl in a swing.

Soon we learned about stenciled quilts and counterpanes (which were light bedspreads). There were also stenciled valances, dust ruffles, curtains, and tablecloths.

We imagined a young woman of the 1825–1840 period wanting to decorate her home—a house with white-washed plaster walls, wide-planked floors, and few windows. She yearned for color and design, but could not afford to buy wallpaper, printed fabrics, or Oriental rugs. What could she do?

Probably she had seen examples of wall stenciling and had learned how the itinerant stencilers did it. Designs were cut out of heavy paper, the paper was pressed against the walls, and paint was then tamped through the designs. Here was a simple process our young homemaker could use. Then she probably stenciled her curtains with flowers and leafy vines and continued by stenciling a valance and a tablecloth. Stenciling was, in fact, both easy and fun, and it brought design and color to simple homes and furnishings. Stenciling became both fashionable and popular in the period 1825–1840. In finishing schools that taught such "polite arts" as needlework, drawing, painting, and music, young women learned to make still-life paintings with stencils, called theorems. They would use a set of stencils, perhaps six in number, to block out on white velvet a plate or basket of fruit and flowers, and then finish it freehand with a brush or pen. Many handsome examples of theorem painting have survived and are prized by collectors today.

Both men and women became professional stencilers working for tinsmiths, who made the popular painted and decorated tinware for dining and kitchen use, and for cabinetmakers, the most famous of them being Lambert Hitchcock of Hitchcocksville (now Riverton), Connecticut.

After 1840, however, the fashion for stenciling ended. Printed fabrics and wallpapers became more generally affordable as industrial production increased and prospered. People papered over their stenciled walls and threw away old stenciled floor-cloths. Men and women who had earned their living by stenciling furniture and tinware turned to new jobs. Only a handful of craftsmen kept the old methods alive and preserved the traditional stencil patterns.

In the years that followed few people were interested in Early American stenciling. But then, in 1918, a woman named Janet Waring of Yonkers, New York, purchased a much-worn set of six Early American stenciled chairs. She tried to restore their subtle patterns with gilt paint and a brush, but soon realized that she could not paint anything even close to the way the patterns had been originally created.

She next tried to find a craftsman to restore her chairs, but she was unsuccessful. She was determined to restore the chairs, and so her great project began: the researching of Early American decoration.[1] She began by searching for craftsmen who were still practicing the old stenciling. She found a few, including George Lord of Portland, Maine.

Miss Waring recalled the circumstances by which she met Lord in 1920: "In Portland, Maine, one day I passed a window filled with stenciled chairs fresh from the hand for which I was searching, for here was the early method of gold stenciling complete in every detail. No gilt paint marred the surface and no wash of umber darkened the sheen of the gold."[2] She went into the shop and began a friendship with George Lord, who was then eighty-seven years old. He had been an apprentice in 1848 at age

1. **Tracing Designs.** In order to trace a pattern, Pat Schad spread her materials carefully over the stenciled and stuffed quilt illustrated in figure 21, page 20. She used clear acetate to trace the designs and then cut the stencils from clear vinyl. Patterns from this quilt appear on pages 21–23. (Courtesy Kelter-Malcé Antiques, New York; photograph by Gail Anderson Myers)

fifteen under Francis Holland at Corey Brothers, chairmakers, in Portland.[3] He was still "painting chair decorations that had changed but little, for he was still using patterns which he had stenciled seventy years before," Miss Waring said.[4]

Lord taught her how to restore her chairs and imparted a wealth of information about Early American decoration. By the time Lord died in 1928, he had trained his apprentice well.

Miss Waring continued to work alone, collecting patterns, writing a book on both wall and furniture stenciling, stenciling furniture and other objects, and occasionally exhibiting her work.

It was about this time, in the 1930s, that a group of artists and collectors began to recognize the true value of the many types of American folk art. The Museum of Modern Art in New York City presented in 1932 a significant exhibition entitled "American Folk Art: The Art of the Common Man in America 1750–1900," including theorems, paintings on glass, naïve paintings, cigar-store Indians, ship figureheads, weathervanes, and cast-iron figures. In his catalogue essay Holger Cahill, who was curator of the exhibition, said that the art was "fresh and original, and at its best an honest and straightforward expression of the spirit of the

A True Friend is the best Possession~ Ben Franklin

people."[5] Authorities were soon hailing the American folk arts as important products of the new American democracy, distinctive for a power, originality, and beauty that rivaled the academic arts.[6]

Miss Waring remained a quiet scholar pursuing her special interest in stenciling, and she was surprised at the success of her book *Early American Stencils on Walls and Furniture* when it was published in 1937.[7]

When she died in 1941, it was learned that she had willed her collection to The Metropolitan Museum of Art and to the Society for the Preservation of New England Antiquities together with an endowment with which to catalogue and preserve it.[8]

As a result of the new interest in American folk arts, collectors and museums began to collect fine examples of stenciling, including bedcovers, usually made of muslin or homespun cotton.

Stenciled quilts and coverlets are rare because they were not produced in shops, as was most stenciled tin and furniture, but by individuals for use in their own homes.

All would live long, but none would be old~ Ben Franklin

Who made these rare stenciled quilts and counterpanes? Perhaps a woman who wished to imitate the look of appliqué work without the tedious needlework or a woman who wanted to use the stencils she had already used to make a theorem. Perhaps it was a woman who had already stenciled curtains or a tablecloth and was so pleased with the results that she decided to stencil a bedcover.

However, only a few women did complete such a project, and the pieces they made were used and laundered to the extent that relatively few examples remain today. Those that have survived probably were only used as the "best spread."

Ten years ago less than twenty-five stenciled bedcovers were known. We now know of more than thirty, and many of them are delightful works of applied art. Most date, of course, from 1825 to 1840, but we were lucky in discovering a more recent example that was made in the period 1880–1910 (see fig. 45). In this book we have included pictures of twenty-two stenciled bedcovers, many previously unpublished. We were allowed to trace patterns from eight of them, and the patterns are included in this book.

We are enjoying a grand revival of stenciling, this time using modern materials that are easy to clean up and inexpensive, so once again people are stenciling walls, curtains, floors, and yes, even quilts.

Margot Strand Jensen made the lovely stenciled and printed spread in figure 3 in 1979, when she was living in Riner, Virginia. It is called *Yard Quilt* and on it she used stenciling, block printing,

Hospitality consists in a little fire, a little food and an immense quiet ~ Emerson

2. **Stenciling for a Child.** You can use Early American patterns, stenciled on a wall and on other objects, to give a warm country feeling to a child's room. Here we stenciled an inexpensive toy chest-and-bench combination from an un-painted-furniture store. Chapter six contains special patterns for children (you work right from this book), and chapter nine provides easy directions for how to stencil *anything*.

3. **Old Crafts Used Today.** This stenciled and printed spread, called *Yard Quilt*, was designed and made in the Medallion style by Margot Strand Jensen in 1979 when she was living in Riner, Virginia. 78″ by 64″. In this piece the artist used the classic techniques of stenciling, block printing, piecing, and quilting, and made a beautiful and lively work of art. (Collection of the artist; photograph courtesy the artist.)

Life, liberty and the pursuit of happiness Declaration of Independence

piecing, and quilting. She created a beautiful and lively contemporary work of art.[9]

Why is there a stenciling revival today?

Perhaps it is a reaction to the high-tech era we now live in; people are using stenciling to put their own unique touches on the objects that surround them at home.

Perhaps it is due to their admiration for the materials and designs of the past, or a nostalgia for the past when times appear to have been simpler to live in. For example, we have found people recreating New England saltbox houses throughout the United States.

An excellent reason for the revival of stenciling is that it is an easy craft that everyone can master—even the Avowed Unartistic—and that is what this book is all about.

By using such modern materials as wax paper and clear vinyl plastic, it is inexpensive to make stencils. Also, modern water-base paints are quick and easy to apply, yet permanent when dry and easy to clean up. So, armed with a few items from your local hardware, hobby, and variety stores even *you* can be a stenciler.

Select an old tray or any unfinished piece you wish to decorate. Choose an appropriate pattern from this book and carefully follow the instructions provided. You will find that stenciling has classic simplicity and quick fulfillment. *And* it is fun! Soon you will be eager to go on to bigger projects, as suggested in this book.

Proclaim liberty unto all the inhabitants thereof

INCLUDED IN THIS BOOK ARE:

▶ More than one hundred Early American stencils from fabric, furniture, and tin, including patterns from Janet Waring's personal collection.

▶ A gallery of twenty-two fine Early American stenciled quilts and coverlets, including patterns from eight of them.

▶ Special sections of patterns for decorating children's rooms and country kitchens.

▶ Step-by-step coaching on how to stencil.

▶ Techniques peculiar to stenciling.

▶ Tips on easy stenciling.

▶ The stories of Janet Waring and Esther Stevens Brazer, prominent stencilers.

Happy stenciling!

Chapter Two

EARLY AMERICAN TREASURES: THE STENCILED QUILT AND COVERLET

Women were expert needleworkers in Early American times. When a woman began a complex quilt, which demanded hours of complicated work, she often started another quilt at the same time. The second was intended for relaxation![1] The complicated quilt had to be worked on by daylight, but she could work on her second quilt by candlelight and not waste precious time.[2] She might also have produced the fabric for the quilt by growing her own flax or cotton. It took sixteen months to produce linen.[3] Or she might have bartered for the fabric with other handiwork or produce from her garden. So the woman who combined her needlework with another art form—stencils and paints—was ambitious indeed! She cut her patterns in heavy paper, which she first oiled so it wouldn't absorb the paint. Many designs on Early American stenciled quilts and coverlets have fine lines—the stems of flowers, for example—so this involved very skillful cutting of the paper.

She made her own paints or bought them from a peddler or by mail. They were unpredictable and hard to use, so first she practiced with them.

Then came the day when she placed her first stencil on the fabric and tamped paint through the holes. She used one stencil for each color, allowing time for the paint to dry if applied over the same spot. This was a critical step for she could not see through her stencils to insure proper placement. (Thanks to clear vinyl, we are able to see through our stencils today.) She had to remember to wipe the stencils often to keep paint from getting underneath.

And how, one wonders, did she manage to keep little fingers away from her paints and brushes? Don't forget: this woman not only had children, but she had a house to run, food to preserve for winter, a garden to tend.

Stenciling a quilt was a lengthy process, and when finished, only part of the job had been accomplished, for then she had to use her needles and thread.

Perhaps she had a patchwork pincushion, very popular in Early American days, or a tomato-shaped pin cushion with a small strawberry attached that was filled with emery powder to keep her needles sharp and rustless. The emery kept the needles from snagging or staining her fabric. Quilters often kept needles threaded with left-over thread in the pincushions, so as not to waste any thread.[4]

So the stenciler took up her favorite needle. Some quilters liked one that had developed a curve from being forced up and down through the fabric. The favorite needle was always the slimmest possible to leave the smallest possible hole, but one strong enough not to break.[5]

One Needle for Twenty-six Years!

"My great-aunt used her needle for twenty-six years and when the threads wore through the eye, put on it a rose made of sealing wax and wore it as a stickpin for the rest of her life," wrote Rose Wilder Lane.[6]

Mrs. Lane was the daughter of Laura Ingalls Wilder, who wrote the *Little House* books about her girlhood on the frontier. Was she talking about gay Aunt Eliza who spent Christmas with the Ingalls in the Big Woods of Wisconsin or was it one of her Wilder aunts, who left a comfortable farm in upstate New York to homestead in southern Minnesota? Mrs. Wilder didn't say, but undoubtedly this aunt was an expert with the needle she so carefully preserved.

A woman's needle was more than just an instrument to get thread into her quilt. "It was her duty, her comfort, her companion, her mode of self-expression," wrote Beth Gutcheon.

4. **Early American Patterns.** Alice Fjelstul used patterns from an 1825–1835 stenciled spread owned by the Museum of American Folk Art in New York City to make this quilt. The lap quilt at the foot of the bed is also contemporary. Photograph by Gary Mortensen, Minneapolis Institute of Arts.

"And when she undertook a project of that magnitude she was not just passing time or doing a bit of show-off needlework, she was making a statement about herself: about her skill, her patience, her ability to endure endless days of hard work and tedium for the sake of the pattern of the whole, and ultimately of her sense of her own value as a human being."[7]

And so our stenciler began to quilt.

The quilting pattern itself was different from the stencil designs, and required precise stitching and absolute accuracy. It might have been a simple overall diamond pattern or a more elaborate scheme combining several quilting patterns.

Caroline Bayles's stenciled quilt in figure 19 has elegant patterns stenciled on large diamonds alternating with all-white diamonds quilted with hyacinths, tulips, roses, and variations. Each block has its own design. It is a magnificent piece.

"Very fine American quilting prides itself on two things," wrote Patsy and Myron Orlofsky in their landmark book on

quilting entitled *Quilts in America.* "First, the stitches and the spaces between should be absolutely even and as small as possible, and the stitches on the back should be as even as those on the front—a very demanding criterion because of the thickness of the material between. Second, it should be impossible to discover where each thread began and ended; the end must not be secured with knots or backstitching that will show."[8]

Our stenciler sewed with one hand under the quilt and soon developed pocked finger tips and a hard callous from her needle.

Why did an Early American needlewoman choose to stencil a coverlet?

One reason was to decorate a piece that was meant to be a light summer spread or a "best spread," not to be used for warmth. Also called a counterpane, it was definitely not an object to wrap up in if you got a chill!

Perhaps she used stencils and paints because she had imagined

5. **Stenciling.** Alice Fjelstul stencils patterns from an Early American counterpane owned by Strawbery Banke Museum in Portsmouth, New Hampshire. The entire spread and patterns from it are illustrated in figures 51–58. Photograph by Gary Mortensen.

a design so fanciful, complex, and colorful that she did not have the fabric or the skill to create the design with the appliqué technique.

Whether she made a stenciled coverlet or a quilt, what she produced was a great personal accomplishment. Those that survived were loved and revered for generations, and have acquired the rich patina that only age, use, washings, and sun can give. The whites have usually become ivory or pale beige.

You will notice this in the gallery of stenciled quilts and coverlets that follows. As you study these rare pieces, you will find that some design traditions used in conventional Early American quilts also appear in some of these pieces, for example, the deliberate error created to divert the "evil eye," analogous to the Oriental idea that to make a perfect thing was to imitate the Deity, therefore unlucky and presumptuous.[9]

One of the stenciled quilts has a deliberate error you will spot easily. It is the One Patch stenciled quilt from Shelburne (see fig. 9). The maker used a different fabric for one patch. She used blue-and-white material for all patches except for the one in the lower corner, where she used a patch of green and white.

Another quilt tradition was to sew hearts and doves on a bride's quilt. There are hearts quilted into the Shelburne One Patch quilt.

Of course, the heart is the universal symbol of love, and in the early 1800s the dove was the symbol of femininity and conjugal felicity.[10]

Block Printing

Professionals block printed counterpanes in Early American times and their craft is often confused with hand stenciling.

In an advertisement in the *Boston Evening Post* of Nov. 16, 1747, John Williams of King Street advised that he would now "stamp" counterpanes and curtains for the same rates as a competitor in the business who was leaving the country.[11]

Printed counterpanes or bedspreads are different from stenciled ones, usually having fewer areas of solid color and more overall patterns. A particularly fine example of a block-printed coverlet is illustrated in figure 7.

6. **Popular Pieced Quilt Pattern.** Early American quilters loved the house pattern used here on a pillow, mirror, and two sconces. You can stencil an ordinary canvas tote bag with a two-color pattern and have a unique gift. Stenciling is fun and easy, and the materials are cheap. See our directions in chapter nine.

7. Excellent example of a block-printed coverlet, c. 1835, region and dimensions unknown. The stamped motifs in this piece are particularly bold and rich. The strong geometrics of the wide border are delightfully complemented by the narrower outside border in a serpentine floral design. (Pivate collection)

8. **Masterpiece.** Stenciled coverlet, unquilted, c. 1830, maker unknown, Utica, New York. 89″ x 81″. The colors are so crisp in this coverlet that it almost seems the artist had only yesterday laid down her stencils, paints, and brushes. Notice the tiny birds circling the center medallion; they also appear in the wide border containing flowers and fruit. (The Metropolitan Museum of Art, New York City; Rogers Fund, 1944)

9. **Purposeful Mistake.** One-patch stenciled and pieced quilt, maker unknown, early 19th century, Connecticut. 90″ x 88″. The maker of this quilt observed an old tradition by using one square of brown calico in the upper left corner, where she should have used a blue one. She chose not to court bad luck by making a "perfect" quilt. In the corners of the calico squares she quilted hearts, so this might have been a wedding piece. (Shelburne Museum, Shelburne, Vermont)

10. **Roses on Diamonds.** Stenciled and pieced quilt, maker unknown, 1825–1840. 80½″ x 81″ (without fringe). The maker of this quilt decorated it with an elegant fishnet fringe. She stenciled roses on 10″ squares, set them on their points in the quilt, and quilted a rosette at the joining of each set of four blocks. (Historic Deerfield, Inc., Deerfield, Massachusetts; photograph by John Giammatteo)

11. **Magnificent Bouquet.** Stenciled counter-pane or bedspread, unquilted, maker unknown, early 19th century, Connecticut or New Jersey. 94″ x 102″. This artist stenciled a wonderful basket of roses and other flowers in the center and an undulating border of roses on her fabric, which was shaped at the bottom to fit a four-poster bed. (The American Museum in Britain, Bath)

12. **Red and White.** Stenciled and pieced quilt. c. 1850, Gales Ferry, Connecticut, 79″ x 90″. Frances Newberry of Gales Ferry in southeast Connecticut made this cheerful quilt. She married Captain Jesse Comstock of nearby Uncasville. The quilt remained in the family until bequeathed by her granddaughter Flore M. Fitch of Noank, Connecticut, to the Lyman Allyn Museum in 1961. (Lyman Allyn Museum, New London, Connecticut)

13. **Twenty Designs.** Stenciled spread, unquilted, maker unknown, c. 1825, New York (?). 100″ x 76½″. The artist who made this piece stenciled beautifully and with a variety of designs. There are many types of flowers, birds, shield-body eagles, weeping willows, two tiny lions, and hearts. (Mr. and Mrs. Foster McCarl, Jr.)

14. **Reverse Stenciling.** Patchwork quilt, initialed R.S.B., c. 1840, Massachusetts, 89″ x 89″. The maker of this quilt stenciled her initials in the center. She used fern, flower, and bird designs, and "splatter work" or reverse stenciling to obtain a shadowy effect. To do reverse stenciling, simply cut your pattern as you would cut out a paper doll, then hold it against your fabric and pounce paint around the edges. (Shelburne Museum)

15. **Primitive.** Stenciled quilt, maker unknown, 1830–1840, 90″ x 86″. The creator of this quilt was truly thinking flowers when she covered this piece so densely with sunflowers. The sunflowers are really charming and must have been enjoyed by others, for the quilt shows wear. Blue is an unusual color for the center flowers; blue was an expensive color in Early American days. (New-York Historical Society, New York City)

16, 16a. **Found in the Attic.** Stenciled spread, un-quilted, maker unknown, 1825–1840, Batavia, New York. 84″ x 84″. In the 1970s, this spread was found stored in the attic of the Holland Land Office Museum, a small museum in Batavia, New York. The stenciler had surely seen wall stenciling, for the border design is a copy of a wall pattern of swags and lighted candles. (Courtesy Holland Land Office Museum, Batavia, New York; photograph by Jim Dusen)

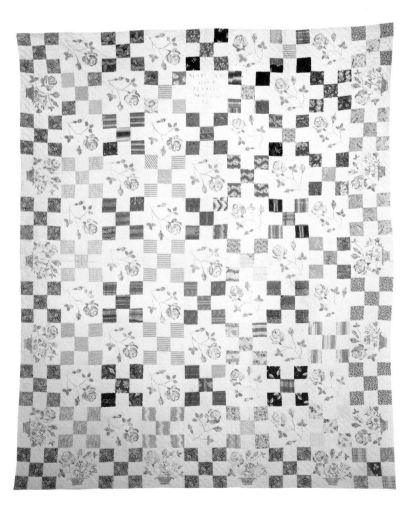

17. **Signed and Dated.** Patchwork and stenciled quilt, made by Mary Ann Hoyt, 1834, Reading, Pennsylvania. 86½″ x 73″. Mary Ann Hoyt signed this piece at the top center, dated it May 15, 1834, and added the words "No. 2, Reading, Pennsylvania." She used the popular open-rose pattern with border designs showing roses and other flowers in blue vases. (The Henry Francis du Pont Winterthur Museum, Winterthur, Delaware)

18. **Peacocks, Parrots, and Fringe.** Stenciled spread, maker M.S.H., 1820–1840, Connecticut. 99½″ x 116″. The artist who created this very beautiful spread painted her initials M.S.H. at the top center, and knotted and plaited elegant fringe. She stenciled peacocks and parrots perched on trees, and bouquets and baskets of flowers. (Shelburne Museum)

19. **Fruit and Flowers.** Stenciled quilt, made by Caroline Bayles McGlasson, c. 1830, Natchez, Mississippi. 92¼" x 70". Caroline Lucinda Bayles, who was born in Natchez, Mississippi, stenciled this vivid quilt. When she was twenty-two, she married Paschel Wilson McGlasson, and they had seven children. Mrs. McGlasson was a marvelous quilter and her designs are excellent. (Dallas Historical Society, Dallas, Texas)

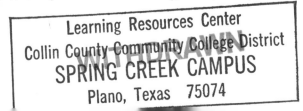

20. **Masterpiece.** Stenciled spread, unquilted, made by Emily Morton, 1826, Thorndyke, Maine. 103″ x 104″. When Emily Morton completed this piece in 1826, she had created one of the masterpieces of Early American stenciling. Her intricate designs are exquisite and her stenciling is extremely well done. (Abby Aldrich Rockefeller Folk Art Center, Williamsburg, Virginia)

Chapter Three

PATTERNS FROM EIGHT STENCILED QUILTS AND COVERLETS

In the pages that follow we illustrate eight great quilts and coverlets, and reproduce patterns taken from them. The designs are shown actual size, *unless otherwise indicated.* Also they are rendered in the original colors, *except where noted.*

Use the patterns to decorate your own quilt or coverlet, or perhaps on a dust ruffle, on curtains, on throw pillows, or to brighten up a spread or a chair.

As you work with the patterns, you will soon realize, as we did, that the designs have vigor, delicacy, and charm—even after more than 150 years. They are still inspiring today. Enjoy them!

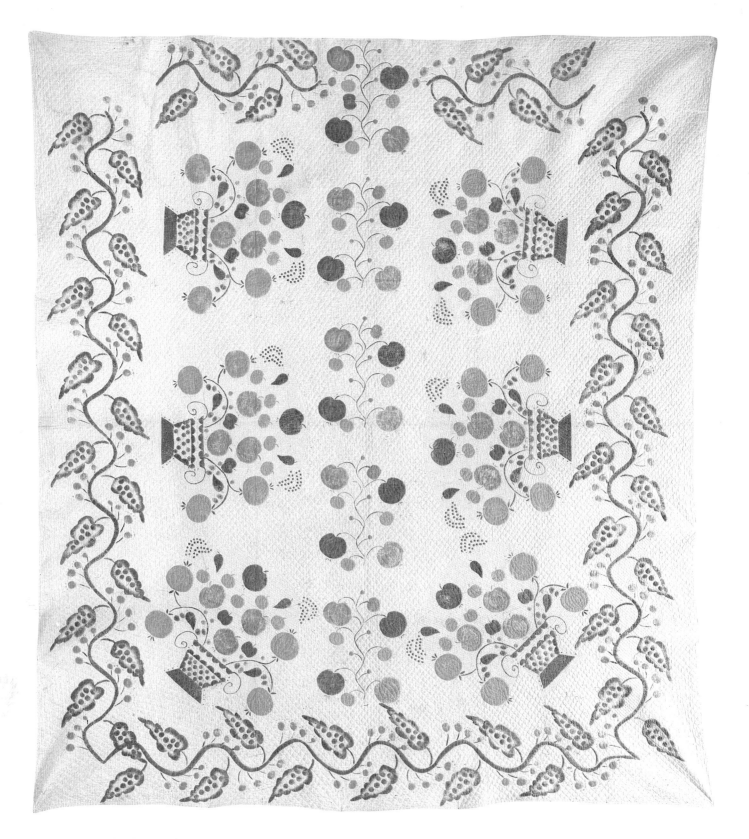

21. **Fruit in Ice Cream Colors.** Stenciled and stuffed-work quilt, 1820–1840. Maker and region unknown. 85″ x 74½″.
The artist used six large blue latticework baskets and filled them with fruit in unconventional colors for a stenciled
piece—pink, yellow, and blue. Her border is also unusual: a large, leafy grapevine with dots inside the leaves,
reminiscent of appliqué pieces known as Martha's Vineyard quilts. The fruit is made with stuffed work, a technique
called trapunto, which brings the designs into relief. Trapunto is done by outlining a design in running stitches and
padding it from the underside. (Kelter-Malcé Antiques, New York City)

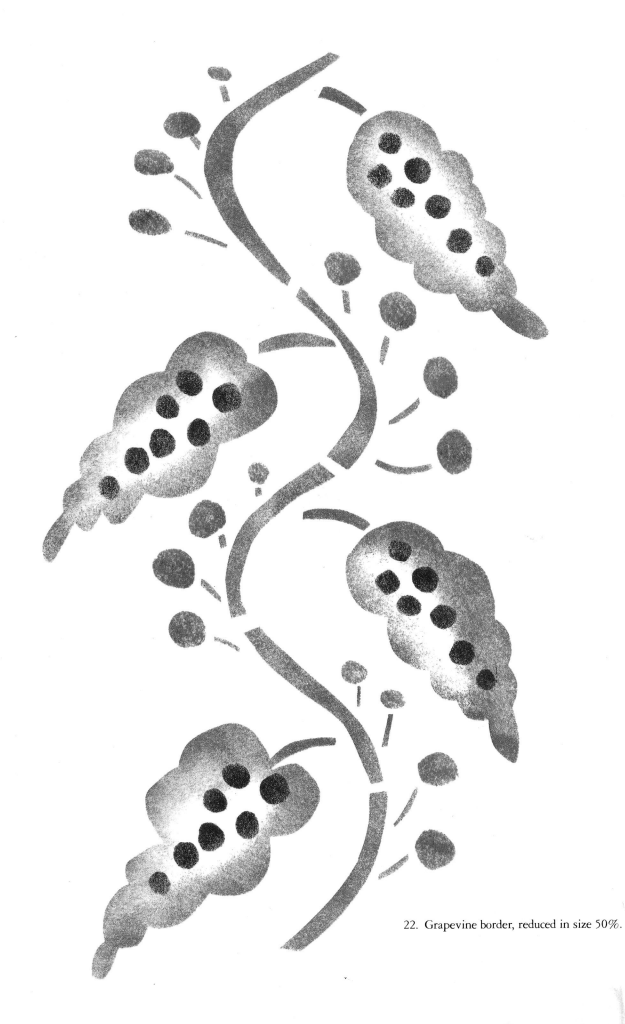

22. Grapevine border, reduced in size 50%.

23. Fruit basket, reduced in size 60%.

24. **Signed on the Back.** Stenciled counterpane, unquilted, made by Hannah Corbin, 1820–1840, Woodstock, Connecticut. 100″ x 94″. Hannah Corbin's coverlet is stenciled with delicate designs in salmon, green, and gold, an unusual color combination. (Old Sturbridge Village, Sturbridge, Massachussets; photograph by Henry E. Peach)

25. Flower medallion and floral motif.

26. Vine and flower border.

27. Medallion and spray of flowers.

28. Flower sprays and vase of flowers.

29. **Vase Bursting with Flowers.** Stenciled bedspread, unquilted, maker unknown, 1825–1835, New England. 91⅜″ x 86″. The artist stenciled a vase with a massive bouquet of flowers in the center of this spread. This piece is cleverly designed and expertly stenciled. (Museum of American Folk Art, New York City; gift of George E. Schoellkopf)

30. Rose tree.

31. Vase.

32. Bouquet for the vase.

33. Three flowers to complete the bouquet in figure 32. The top two flowers go on the sides, as partially seen in figure 32. The bottom flower attaches to the end of the middle stems on both right and left; see figure 29.

34. Elements of the massive bouquet at the center of the spread, using the vase in figure 31 as the base.

35. Elements of the massive bouquet at the center of the spread, using the vase in figure 31 as the base.

36. **Maple Leaves.** Stenciled quilt, maker unknown, 1840–1850, probably Vermont. 90½″ x 88¾″. This quilt was purchased more than fifty years ago at an auction in Essex Junction, Vermont, by the mother of the present owner. It is a lovely piece and very different from the usual fruit and flower-basket motifs. (Mrs. Robert Keegan, Hudson, Ohio; photograph by Roland Gamble)

37. Maple-leaf border.

38. Star.

39. **Acorn Tree, Plums.** Stenciled bedspread, unquilted, made by Lucinda Howland; the stenciling was done by an unidentified neighbor, c. 1831, Lisle, Broome County, New York. 86″ x 81½″. When Lucinda Howland was married in 1831, she made this spread and asked a neighbor to stencil it. We included a few designs from it in our first book *Early American Wall Stencils in Color*, and here we present several more, including a charming acorn tree. (Cortland County Historical Society, Cortland, New York)

40. Acorn tree.

41. Pears.

42. Lemon tree.

43. Plums.

44. Flowers (colors are not original).

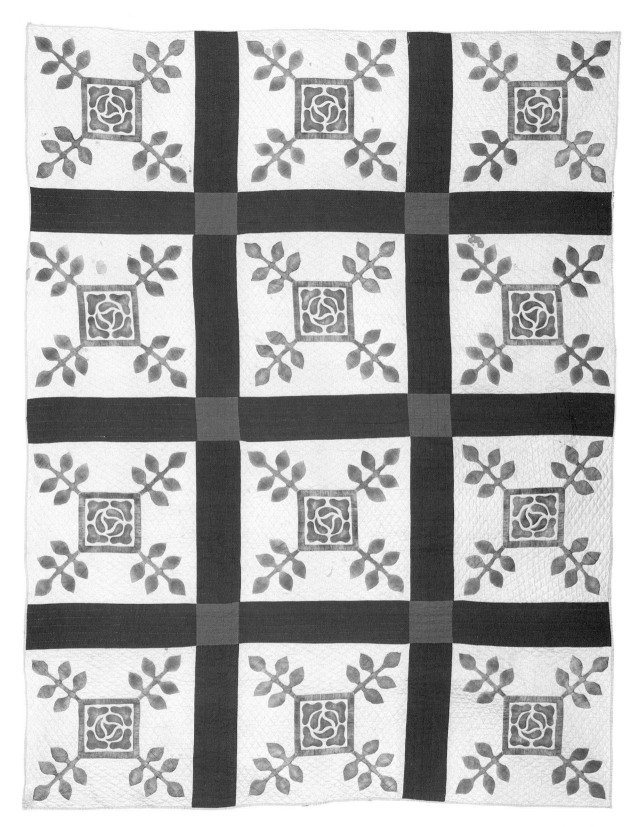

45. **From Illinois.** Stenciled and appliqué quilt, maker unknown, 1880–1910, found in Ladd, Illinois. 89″ x 68″. This quilt, of a later era, was found in northern Illinois in a coal-mining region settled by people from Scranton, Pennsylvania. The maker stenciled a dozen abstract roses and appliquéd them in thin brown frames, with leaves radiating from the corners. The quilting lines converge at the corners of each rose panel. (Nancy Hannah, Minneapolis, Minnesota; photograph by Gary Mortensen)

46. Sprig of leaves.

47. Abstract rose in frame.

48, 48a. **Wonderful Stitching.** Stenciled quilt, maker and region unknown, c. 1850. 83″ x 78″. The quilting in this piece is especially handsome. (The Edison Institute: Greenfield Village and Henry Ford Museum, Dearborn, Michigan; photograph by Rudy Ruzicska)

49. Bird.

50. Rose, bud, and leaves.

51. **Theorems, an Eagle, and House.** Stenciled counterpane, unquilted, maker unknown, 1825–1840, probably New Hampshire. 95″ x 94½″. The maker of this counterpane stenciled four large theorems, a shield-body eagle (symbol of the young United States), and a house. (Strawbery Banke, Portsmouth, New Hampshire)

52. (Opposite). House with blue fence. This and the following stencil patterns from the Strawbery Banke counterpane are made with the swirling technique of stenciling, which is also called rouging.

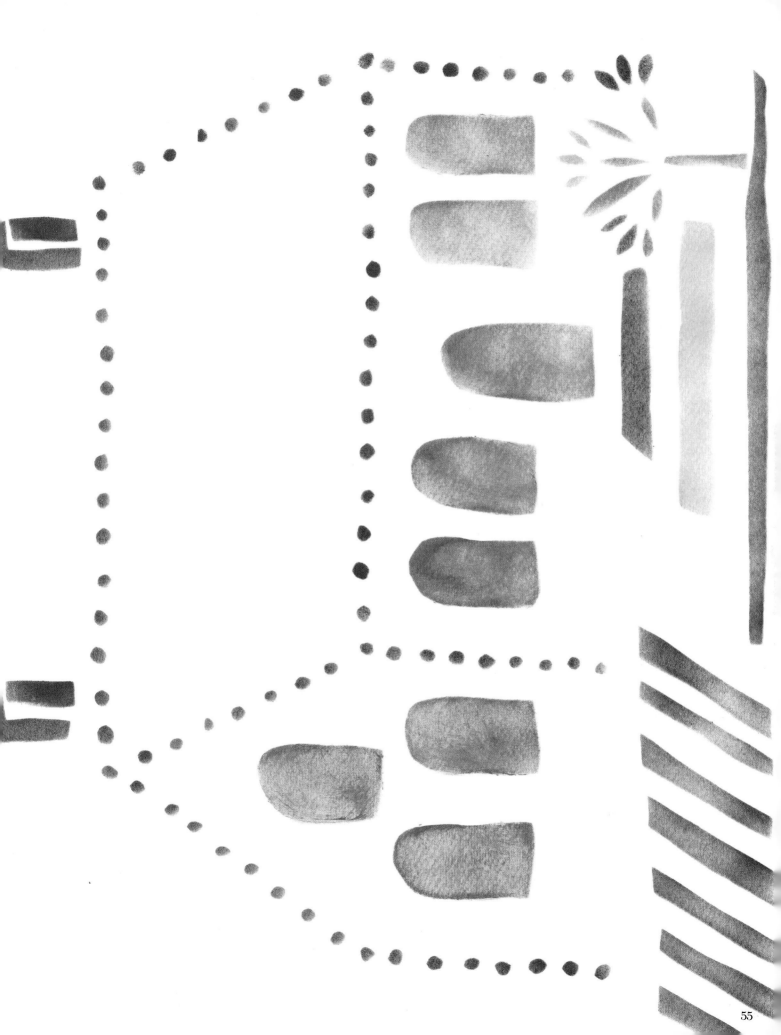

53. Shield-body eagle.

54. Urn with flowers.

55. Vine with bird from left side of house.

56. Another vine with bird from right side of house.

57. Thistle.

58. Flower made with hearts, and an oak leaf.

Chapter Four

STENCILS FROM FURNITURE AND TIN; ALSO THE WORK OF ESTHER STEVENS BRAZER

What a noisy, busy, fascinating place an Early American tin-smith's shop was! When a tin stenciler went to work, her daughter loved to visit, for there were shiny bits of discarded tin everywhere to play with. Of course, the child begged to keep a few, promising to be careful of the sharp edges. What wonderful things she could make with the tin scraps! If she was tall enough to use the turning machine, then she could fold the raw edges into a hem and thus make a little mirror for her doll.[1]

Then she might go to the table where her mother and the other painters were working. They stenciled coffeepots; teapots; sugarbowls; cannisters; sconces; trays (called *waiters*); *trunks*, which were storage or document boxes that children often used as lunch boxes; bread trays; and a purely American utensil with a most delightful shape—square apple dishes with high curved sides.[2] With their stencils they painted gay designs of fruit and flowers, vines, leaves, birds, people, and landscapes in Chinese vermilion, Prussian blue, chrome, King's yellow, white lead, and drop lake (a purplish red), combined with gold and bronze powders.[3]

The NOISE! There was the banging of the mallets as the tinsmiths in big aprons shaped the tinplate over the molds, and the squealing and rasping of their files on the tin, and the clatter of the tinware itself. No wonder the business earned the nickname "Bang-all"!

The SMOKE! There was a blue haze in the air from the solder as it bubbled in the soldering boiler.

The SMELLS! There were the odors from the japan paints, turpentine, and varnish, which was mixed and cooked over an open fire.

It was hot in the shop, too. The painted tin was baked or "stoved" in an oven after it was painted and again after it was varnished.

The child was soon shooed out of the shop so her mother could return to work, for there was a great demand for the gaily painted tin. It was a refreshing change in Early American kitchens from the usual somber iron, pewter, and wood.[4] Also, it was easier to handle and much easier to clean.[5]

Is it surprising that women worked professionally as tin painters in Early American times? They also worked as stencilers in furniture shops, and in a chair factory owned by Lambert Hitchcock in Hitchcocksville, Connecticut, near Barkhamsted in northwestern Connecticut.

Records from tinsmiths show that the women painters were paid from $1.25 to $2 a week, in a time when materials were expensive. Brushes were $1 and the best varnish was $10 a quart.[6]

A devoted scholar of the Early American tin industry, Shirley Spaulding DeVoe of Bridgewater, Connecticut, has found the names of approximately thirty women who stenciled and japanned tin, furniture, and the faces of clocks.

These artists used japan paints, which were oil-base paints with a high percentage of japan drier, which enabled them to dry faster than other oil paints.

The artists very seldom signed a piece, but if they did, it was probably with tiny initials in some discreet spot.

Hepzibah Wilcox probably signed a black japan coffee pot decorated with gold leaf when she worked in a tin shop in Berlin, Connecticut, in 1818. The initials "H.W." were marked on this particular piece of tin, and Mrs. DeVoe has found records that Miss Wilcox worked in the shop before her marriage.[7]

In one instance we know that a woman did more than just paint. Mrs. Sarah Greenleaf Upson was part owner of several tin shops in the 1830s and 1840s. She painted tinware for the shops in addition to keeping house and raising five children, and when she and her husband bought an interest in a clock company, she managed a group of young women who decorated the iron clock-cases.[8]

Tinsmithing was a thriving industry for small dooryard and cottage tinshops from the early 1800s until about 1850. Peddlers carried their products westward with the expanding country and north into Canada. In the middle of the nineteenth century, however, people came to prefer new styles in kitchen and tableware, such as Britannia Ware, and silver-plated and copper articles with pewter mountings.[9]

Larger shops and mills began to produce these objects and they also manufactured tin. Many grew into factories. The tinware was now machine stamped with designs. Most of the small shops that employed the women painters went out of business.[10]

Stenciled furniture also went out of style about the mid 1800s. People preferred furniture that showed the grain of the wood and carved pieces became popular. Only a few stencilers continued using the old techniques.

More than seventy years later, in 1921, a young woman named Esther Stevens Frazer set out to discover the original techniques of stenciling. She and her husband had just bought an old house in Cambridge, Massachusetts, and she decided to restore it and decorate it in the styles of the early 1800s. She was surprised to discover that there was no information available on how to stencil tin, furniture, and walls, or how to do the wood graining so popular in the period 1815–1845. She found that the most recent painter's guide had been published in 1825, so it had been long out of print!

She spoke to a friend, Homer Eaton Keyes, who was preparing to edit and publish in Boston a new magazine called *The Magazine Antiques.* He told her that little was known about the techniques of the early craftsmen and urged her to study them. He promised to publish her findings in his magazine.[11] So she did.

Years later Mrs. Frazer wrote: "It therefore became necessary for me to learn by analytical observation of the designs themselves through attempting to record the exact effects, and by tracking down odd bits of information in some antique instruction book."[12]

Soon she was tracking down old formulas and experimenting at home with paints, varnish, and stencils. She meticulously recorded her work and collected old patterns wherever she went.[13] Her first article appeared in the April 1922 issue of *Antiques,* the magazine's fourth issue. This was the first of many articles she wrote for the magazine.

She found several of the old craftsmen, including George Lord of Portland, Maine, who was then teaching Janet Waring. Mrs. Frazer had been born in Portland and traced her ancestry back to Paul Revere's father and to Zachariah Brackett Stevens, a tinsmith and tinware entrepreneur in Stevens Plains (now Westbrook), Maine.[14]

Esther Stevens Frazer, who became Esther Stevens Brazer after her second marriage, soon was expert in the Early American techniques: japanning, antiquing, brush-stroke painting, free-hand bronzing, laying gold leaf, finishing, and (in her own words) "floating on color," a technique of flowing transparent color overtones on a pattern, blurring and softening sharp lines into subtle shading.

She taught her methods in Massachusetts. With the developing interest in the American folk arts in the early 1930s, she found her classes growing. In 1937, after her divorce and marriage to Clarence W. Brazer, she moved to an old house in Flushing, Long Island, New York, and continued to teach. One student recalled her devotion to her weekly class in Hartford, Connecticut, about 100 miles from her home. "She left her home at 5 a.m.," said Mrs. Robert Keegan, who was in that class, "drove from Flushing to Manhattan; took the train to Hartford for class, which started at 10:30 A.M.; had a break for lunch; taught all afternoon; ate dinner in Hartford and took the train back to New York in the evening."[15]

Mrs. Brazer's message was that recreating the Early American style is a fine art, requiring time, care, meticulous attention to details, artistic talent, and many materials. She decided that her long years of research and "learning by trial-and-error methods were so costly in time and effort" that she should set what she had learned down in a book.[16] So she compiled her material into the book *Early American Decoration,* which was published in 1940 by the Pond-Ekberg Company of Springfield, Massachusetts.

When Mrs. Brazer died in 1945 at the age of forty-seven, she left loyal followers who wanted to carry on her work and high standards of authentically reproducing the old designs, so nine of them met with her husband Clarence W. Brazer and formed a guild bearing her name.[17]

Today that guild is the Historical Society of Early American Decoration, and it maintains offices and a museum in Albany, New York. The museum has Mrs. Brazer's collections and also objects contributed by her students.

If you are interested in learning much more about these early decorating techniques, contact the Historical Society at 19 Dove Street, Albany, New York, 12210, and ask for printed information and a list of teachers who will help you learn. And prepare yourself for gold leaf, bronzing powders, and ten coats of varnish and rubbing down between coats—authentic to the last squiggle and curlicue.

We have found that with modern products we can reproduce bronzing and silver and gilt in just a fraction of the time and effort the old methods require. We use quick-drying acrylic paints, which clean up easily with water. It is a quick method that is fun, not tedious. People who stencil our way start with one project and then go on and on. One student began with walls and ended stenciling her sneakers!

The Early American patterns in this chapter are taken from tin and furniture. They can be used on tin and furniture, of course, but also on mailboxes, vinyl placemats, paper products, and fabric. We show some patterns in the original colors and others in modern color combinations to spur your imagination. To use them our way, follow the simple directions described in chapter nine.

59. **Checkerboard.** Painted and stenciled checkerboard. 25″ x 14″. (Collection of Patricia Schad; photograph by William Holland)

60. Horse stencil from checkerboard.

61. **Stenciled Chair.** Painted and stenciled chair, maker and region unknown. (Collection of Patricia Schad; photograph by William Holland)

62. Pattern from stenciled chair.

63. **Document Box.** Painted and stenciled tin box. 19″ x 10½″ x 8½″.
(Collection of Patricia Schad; photograph by William Holland)

64. Patterns from box in new colors.

65. **Tin Tray.** Painted and stenciled tin tray with a girl, dog, and a peacock. 17½″ x 24″. (Collection of Patricia Schad; photograph by William Holland)

66. Girl and dog patterns.

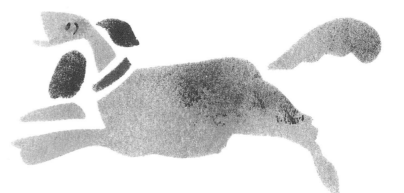

67. **Peacock Cradle.** Painted and stenciled cradle, maker unknown, c. 1850, Bucks County, Pennsylvania. 21″ x 22″ x 41″. (Collection of Paul R. Flack; photograph by William Holland)

68. Patterns from peacock cradle.

69. **Pheasant Tray:** Painted and stenciled tin tray. 17¼" x 24". (Collection of Patricia Schad; photograph by William Holland)

70. Pattern from pheasant tray.

71. **Tin Tray.** Painted and stenciled tin tray with a woman and a man. 19″ x 26″. (Collection of Patricia Schad; photograph by William Holland)

72. Woman and man patterns from the tray.

73. **Three Trays.** Three painted and stenciled trays. (Collection of Patricia Schad; photograph by William Holland)

74. Pattern from octagonal tray (8¾″ x 12″).

75. **Fruit Tray.** Painted and stenciled tray. 9″ x 12″. (Collection of Patricia Schad; photograph by William Holland)

76. Pattern from fruit tray.

77. **Deed Box.** Tin document box. 9¾″ x 8″ x 6¾″. (Collection of Patricia Schad; photograph by William Holland)

78. Pattern from deed box.

79. **Tea Caddy with Tray.** Tin tea caddy. 7″ high x 4½″ diam. (Collection of Patricia Schad; photograph by William Holland)

80. Pattern from tea caddy.

81. **Wooden Box.** Painted and stenciled wooden box. 10½″ x 5¾″ x 7½″. (Collection of Patricia Schad; photograph by William Holland)

82. Pattern from front of box.

83. **Design for Stenciled Crest Rail.** Seashell pattern for a stenciled crest rail, oil paint stenciled on paper. Anonymous artist, c. 1840. (The Metropolitan Museum of Art; Harris Brisbane Dick Fund, 1934)

84. Pattern from crest rail.

85. **Another Pattern for a Crest Rail.** Here is another pattern for a stenciled crest rail. On the opposite page we have broken it into its three different elements to show you how it was constructed. Stencil predominant color first. (Pattern from the Holcomb Collection, Print Department, The Metropolitan Museum of Art)

86. **Two Tin Boxes.** Two painted and stenciled tin boxes. Larger: 9½″ x 6¾″ x 6½″. Smaller: 8″ x 4″ x 4¼″. (Collection of Alice Fjelstul; photograph by Gary Mortensen)

87. Pattern from smaller box.

88. Patterns from larger box. The red in the church windows was painted over the gold paint.

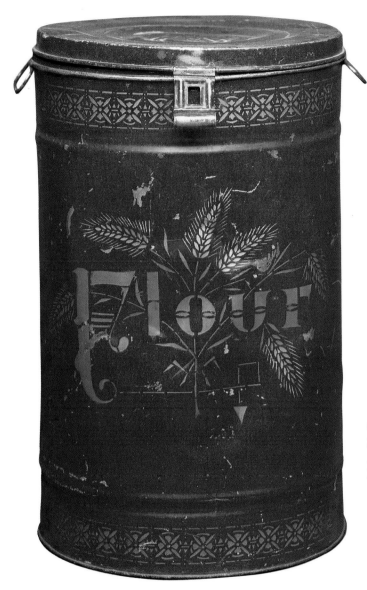

89. **Flour Canister.** Tin flour canister. 20½″ high x 12½″ diam. (Collection of Alice Fjelstul; photograph by Gary Mortensen)

90. Patterns from flour canister.

91. **Spice Boxes.** Tin canister holding seven spice containers. Canister: 3½″ high x 8½″ diam. Containers: 3¼″ high x 2½″ diam. (Collection of Alice Fjelstul; photograph by Gary Mortensen)

92. Pattern from spice containers.

Chapter Five

JANET WARING AND STENCILS FROM HER COLLECTION

A chauffeur from Yonkers, New York, drove a limousine up a dusty country road in New England and stopped at a dilapidated farmhouse, where a farmer was pitching hay from his wagon through an open door. The chauffeur opened the car's back door and out stepped a short, well-dressed woman with a rounded figure. It was the early 1930s and Janet Waring was at work. She walked quickly up to the farmer, followed by her chauffeur and a photographer. She asked the farmer if she could look inside the house, for as she explained, she had researched this house and was looking for old wall-stencil designs.

Once inside, she stepped through the hay the farmer was storing there and examined the walls. She poked them and peeled off layers of wallpaper with the help of the chauffeur. Then she found some dramatic stencil work and set about to photograph them as soon as she had the hay cleared away.

She asked the farmer to take the hay out of the room. He was dumbfounded, and refused. She offered to pay him. He still refused. She offered to pay him for taking the hay out, and then pay him again for putting it back in the room. It was an offer a shrewd New England farmer could not refuse. Such was Janet Waring's unique method of researching Early American stenciling.[1]

In her quest for stenciling Miss Waring was spiritually alone. The farmer thought she was daft. Her sister, Susan B. Waring, waited in the limousine; she often accompanied Janet on the drives, but never got out of the car. The chauffeur and the photographer were, of course, being paid.

At that time almost nothing had been written about stenciling or other Early American folk arts and crafts. The scholarly community, artists, and collectors considered them quaint and naïve—hardly on the level of the academic arts.

And who was willing to travel along remote roads in New England, looking for old stencil patterns? Poking in vacant buildings, visiting small towns, doing research in libraries and village halls, talking to people, cataloguing, photographing, collecting stencils from walls, furniture, and tin, buying groups of old stencils?

The first person who did the job was this determined woman from Yonkers who spent summers in New England in New Marlboro, Massachusetts, a town in the southwest part of the state near the borders with Connecticut and New York.

Janet Waring was the daughter of John T. Waring, a wealthy hat manufacturer, and Jean Baldwin Waring, who was from an old New York family. Miss Waring was a member of the Society of Mayflower Descendants (her father's family had settled Putnam, New York) and was also a member of the Colony Club of New York. She belonged to St. John's Episcopal Church in Yonkers and was active in the women's auxiliaries.

One day in Litchfield, Connecticut, in 1918, when she was about fifty, she purchased a set of six old chairs, which were very worn, and took them home to restore them. She tried painting gilt on the gold fruit and leaves on the broad crest rails, and knew at once that this was the wrong technique.[2] She realized that she would have to find someone to show her how to restore the softly muted designs.

We'll let Miss Waring speak for herself. The following quote is taken from a tattered newspaper clipping that was taped inside a blanket chest she had stenciled. (The chest, now in the collection of Patricia Schad, is illustrated in figure 93.)

"What led to my doing the work," she said, "was the difficulty I had in finding anyone who could restore the much worn chairs I owned myself. The method of the old process seemed to have been quite lost, the reproductions were so unmistakenly reproductions that they were...unsatisfactory. It was then that I determined to try to discover the old process myself, and that has led to many experiences and much information."[3]

Miss Waring went on to say that she had studied with three old craftsmen, one of whom was ninety-seven and "had kept all the cunning of his hand and brain." The second was eighty-five and the third was a painter of trays and bellows.

One of these craftsmen was George Lord of Portland, Maine, mentioned earlier, and he was the first to show her the process of stenciling—not freehand painting with gilt paint. On the day when she walked into his shop, he showed her how to stencil: he spread on the surface of the piece of furniture a thin coat of size compounded of varnish and turpentine to act as a binder to hold the powders that he would apply later. In an hour or two when the adhesive was nearly dried, he used his stencils and brushed on the bronzes with small velvet pads, "modeling the fruits with a dexterous hand," Miss Waring recalled.[4]

From Mr. Lord and the other craftsmen she learned more about stenciling the old way and went on researching Early American techniques and patterns for over twenty years. Indeed, her hobby grew to be the major interest of her life.

Janet Waring traveled many miles on behalf of stenciling, visiting libraries, shops, and old buildings, and she made many friends through her research. She also found some original Early American stencils, which became part of her collection. In a dusty old volume in a cabinetmaker's shop she found more than fifty stencils that had been cut and used by Jarred Johnson of Brush Hill, Sheffield, Massachusetts. She bought the volume. Johnson was a farmer and cabinetmaker who was born in 1801.[5] Interestingly enough, Miss Waring found his exact patterns on a Hitchcock chair she owned.

At an auction a friend of Miss Waring's bought for her several hundred patterns made by Ivers White of Ashburnham, Massa-

93. Janet Waring's Blanket Chest.
Janet Waring, one of the first to research Early American stenciling, painted and stenciled this chest. It has a drawer in the bottom and an unusual drop front; the top lifts up. Miss Waring painted the floral design freehand and stenciled the leaf border. The chest was displayed at The Metropolitan Museum of Art during her lifetime. It remained in Miss Waring's family until 1980. (Collection of Patricia Schad; photograph by William Holland)

94. Janet Waring's Leaf Border. To make this border of leaves, you need bronze and gold acrylic paint. Trace and cut the single leaf at the lower left. Using the bronze acrylic, stencil around the edges to give a shaded effect, leaving the center of the leaf unpainted, as at the lower right. Then, using the gold acrylic, stencil a second leaf overlapping the first. Alternate stenciling leaves in a row. (Be sure to wipe your stencil between paint applications so the colors do not get mixed together.) Finish with a solid leaf at the end. Other color combinations would also be good with this pattern, such as two shades of green (deep hunter green and a yellowish green) or brown and umber.

chusetts, a chair stenciler and a coach painter. He was born in 1804 and died in 1884.[6] In this book we have included patterns from both White and Johnson, and each man's patterns are identified.

She worked comparatively alone in the field until The Museum of Modern Art's show of American folk art was held in 1932. After that, critics and collectors began to hail the American folk arts and crafts, and Miss Waring found interest in stenciling growing. She exhibited some of her work and began compiling her research for a book.

She traveled to Ohio and visited nineteenth-century communities there to see if the early wall stencilers had carried their patterns west with the great movement to the frontiers in the early 1800's. She did not report that she had discovered any.[7]

Janet Waring always wondered if the techniques of stenciling had been brought to New England by settlers from England, and in 1935 she visited Britain to try to locate examples of English wall stenciling, but she found none.[8]

Her book, *Early American Stencils on Walls and Furniture,* was publishing in 1937 by William R. Scott, Inc. In it, she described wall stenciling in eighty houses, illustrating her text with many black-and-white photographs. She also discussed stenciling on furniture and tin.

Miss Waring was praised for the high quality of her scholarship and for meticulously capturing an important early craft that had nearly been obliterated. The wall stenciling part of her book was reprinted. Her publisher said he got 500 letters from people who had stenciled their walls using the book!

Was There Wall Stenciling in England?

When Miss Waring went to England in 1935, she found stenciling on tin, furniture, wallpaper, and rood screens (used in churches as dividers), but no wall stenciling.

Several years later, after her book was published, she learned of a person in England who had found some examples. She sent a copy of her book to Francis W. Reader, and in return he told her that he had found about ten different wall stencils in Buckingham, Gloucestershire, Essex, and Kent Counties.[9]

British stenciling had characteristics similar to American patterns, according to Mr. Reader: floral motifs, stripe designs, and reeded or entwined pilasters, but these were also characteristics of wallpapers of the time. Judging by the number of his examples from the early 1800s, he concluded that wall stenciling was quite common in England at that time, which was the same period it was common in New England. In more recent years several more examples have been reported.[10]

The limited number of examples found in Britain indicates that wall stenciling was probably not as pervasive as it was in New England, and that it did not develop with the individuality and vitality typical of American wall stenciling.

What was Janet Waring like? William R. Scott, her publisher, remembers her as "lots of fun, bubbling over with enthusiasm, particularly about stencils of any kind....She was short, ample and possessed of a piercing eye that was usually twinkling."[11]

Janet Waring's great-niece, Barbara Hunt Smith, recalls visiting her home in Yonkers, where she lived with her sister Susan, and watching her work. Mrs. Smith said that her Aunt Janet was "bouncy, full of energy, pleasant and delightful to visit and didn't sit in the parlor and wait for tea." Aunt Janet was "totally preoccupied with her work" and many times invited her niece up to her studio, which consisted of several rooms on the top floor of the house. The rooms were filled with her work—stenciled furniture and boxes—and her materials—gold leaf and powders. "She was a perfectionist," Mrs. Smith recalled. "Cutting her stencils was remarkable to see." Describing her physically, Mrs. Smith said that her Aunt Janet was a "short, chubby person in a family of tall thin people."[12]

As Janet Waring and her sister Susan grew older, they discussed the future of her stencil collection. They decided that after her death, it should go to two places: the Society for the Preservation of New England Antiquities in Boston and The Metropolitan Museum of Art in New York City. They made arrangements for this bequest and left funds providing for more than 2,000 pieces of the collection to be duplicated so that a set went to each institution, with the originals going to the SPNEA. Janet Waring died January 18, 1941, when she was about seventy.

In 1954, her collection was duplicated at the Metropolitan's print department. The original tracings were sent to the SPNEA with one complete photostatic set; the Metropolitan kept the second set.[13] We have searched through Waring's collection at both museums and have selected the strongest patterns for this book.

Many of the designs were cut by William Eaton of Boston, who was considered the best of the old stencilers in New England by George Lord of Portland, Maine. As a boy, Lord had known Eaton and admired his work. He watched him cut his designs; no pattern was too intricate for Eaton's knife. Once young Lord asked Eaton for one of his stencils, but the older man refused, saying his employers would object.[14]

Many years later Waring came across six dusty folios of stencils in the corner of a loft of a furniture stenciler and she purchased them from him. She knew they were William Eaton's stencils for his name or initials were cut in many of the patterns. The next day she took them to Mr. Lord who went through the stencils one whole afternoon. She let him trace as many as he wished. He did not mention if one was the stencil he had coveted long ago.[15]

You also will love the Eaton designs, because they have a charming Currier and Ives flavor to them. See examples in figure 109.

Janet Waring, who loved these stencil patterns, called her work "a pleasure and an adventure."[16] Surely she would be pleased to know that the patterns are once again available. Enjoy them!

Meanwhile, her book is still in print. It is truly a landmark work on American stenciling. Her name has become permanently associated with the craft she loved.[17]

95. Flowers, crest-rail stencils. (Janet Waring Collection, Print Department, The Metropolitan Museum of Art)

96. Crest-rail stencils by William Eaton. (Janet Waring Collection, The
Metropolitan Museum of Art)

97. Wall stencils by Xenophon Cleveland. (Janet Waring Collection, Society for the Preservation of New England Antiquities, Boston, Massachusetts—hereinafter referred to as SPNEA)

98. and 99. Crest-rail patterns by Ivers White. The gray areas show the overlap of the stencils. (Janet Waring Collection, SPNEA)

100. Assorted stencils. (Janet Waring Collection, SPNEA).

101. Borders. The center design in gold has been
repeated in green and pink on the right. (Janet
Waring Collection, SPNEA)

102. Crest-rail designs by William Eaton. (Janet Waring Collection, The Metropolitan Museum of Art)

103. Crest-rail design by William Eaton. (Janet Waring Collection, The Metropolitan Museum of Art)

104. Leaf designs by Jarred Johnson. (Janet Waring Collection, SPNEA). Tree design by Jarred Johnson. (Janet Waring Collection, The Metropolitan Museum of Art)

105. Wall stencils from Waring's Copley Collection. (SPNEA)

106. Design of landscape containing church, houses, and figures, Cutting and Morrill Collection. Cutting and Morrill were chair manufacturers in Albany, New York, c. 1851. (The Metropolitan Museum of Art)

107. Leaf designs. (Janet Waring Collection, SPNEA)

Chapter Six

STENCILS FOR CHILDREN'S ROOMS

A child in Colonial times usually had a small stark space in which to sleep. It was always shared with brothers and sisters.

The space was probably a loft or a small room off the kitchen that also served as a borning room. In George Washington's childhood home on a farm near Fredericksburg, Virginia, there were six rooms in the house, four below and two above, into which were crowded thirteen beds and a couch![1]

If an Early American mother wanted to bring color and design into her child's sleeping area, she might well have done it with stencils. She might have stenciled the ever-popular roses and leaves on off-white homespun curtains. The same designs might have been applied to the back slats of simple painted chairs.

Today, if you're short on time, you can decorate inexpensively for your child by using stencils cut with Early American patterns.

They will bring a warm country look to your little person's room.

You need only a few items from your local hobby and fabric shops. You will want to use acrylic paints which wash up with water and are permanent when dry. You will want to cut your designs in clear heavy vinyl. Following our directions for stenciling is easy and fun.

You can bring color and design to plain store-bought curtains and to an inexpensive spread. Apply the designs also to scatter pillows, to a toy chest purchased from a store stocking unpainted furniture, to a plastic wastepaper container, and to the border of a bulletin board.

Now you've got a whole new look to the room.

We feel sure the following patterns will spur you to action. Most of them are from the Janet Waring Collection.

108. Horses. Top design from Janet Waring Collection, SPNEA; bottom design from Cutting and Morrill Collection, The Metropolitan Museum of Art. (Opposite). Horse patterns by Ivers White. The top pattern was a tin stencil. (Janet Waring Collection, SPNEA)

109. Nautical designs by William Eaton. (Janet Waring Collection, SPNEA and The Metropolitan Museum of Art)

110. Circus animals and a train. Designs enlarged. Animal stencils by James W. Preston of Newark, New Jersey, 1858. (Janet Waring Collection, The Metropolitan Museum of Art)

111. Deer, a fish, and a cow. (Janet Waring Collection, The Metropolitan Museum of Art)

112. (Opposite). Minstrel man by William Eaton. This is an example of reverse stenciling. (Janet Waring Collection, SPNEA)

Chapter Seven

STENCILS FOR A COUNTRY KITCHEN FROM THE JANET WARING COLLECTION

"Hospitality consists in a little fire, a little food and an immense quiet," wrote Ralph Waldo Emerson.

Your kitchen is where your food and hospitality begin, and you can use old patterns there to give a feeling of Early American comfort and welcome. You'll be surprised to find how some old things you were ready to discard can be made to look fresh and immensely appealing by decorating them with stencils.

Spruce up old canisters and trays for use and display. The same patterns can be stenciled on white muslin for inexpensive curtains. Then use the patterns on a set of potholders to hang next to your oven. Most of the patterns are from the Janet Waring collection.

113. Stencil from the lid of a wooden butter box. The original is in black.
(Private collection)

114. Melons, cherries, and a pumpkin. Melons and pumpkin by Ivers White; cherries by George Lord. (Janet Waring Collection, SPNEA)

115. Pears and a pineapple. Stencils found in Lee, Massachusetts. (Janet Waring Collection, SPNEA)

116. Lemon and berries by George Lord. (Janet Waring Collection, SPNEA)

117. Grapes by George Lord. (Janet Waring Collection, SPNEA)

118. Basket and flowers by Ivers White. (Janet Waring Collection, SPNEA)

119. Vase and flowers. Vase is by Ivers White. (Janet Waring Collection, SPNEA). Floral spray. (Janet Waring Collection, The Metropolitan Museum of Art)

120. Flower designs. Morning glory. (Janet Waring Collection, The Metropolitan Museum of Art). Other flower patterns. (Janet Waring Collection, SPNEA)

121. Flowers. (Janet Waring Collection, SPNEA)

Chapter Eight

THEOREMS

A *man* painting theorems!

Traditionally, it was women who made those pictures on white velvet of baskets and bowls filled with fruit and flowers, glowing with vivid color. They used stencils for blocking out the subject, and then finished it freehand. Theorem painting was a regular course of study in schools for young women, taught right along with the needle arts and other "polite occupations."

But in 1832 there was a man who took lessons in theorem painting and enjoyed them so much that he continued to paint theorems as a hobby. He lived in Georgetown, now part of the District of Columbia, and wrote about his hobby in his diary when he was twenty-four. He was an artist and a successful businessman in later years in Rochester, New York. He was unidentified in the source of our information: *The Magazine Antiques* for June 1932.

On Sunday, April 22, 1832, he wrote: "Verry [sic] pleasant and warm. I went down to Alexandria to take a lesson on painting on velvit [sic] and finished two pieces and it was said to be the handsomest…in Georgetown."[1] Almost a year later he wrote: "Last night I painted a piece of fruit on velvit [sic] and completed it, and think to paint a gar [garland?] of flowers tonight, they are about ½ yard square."

He planned to have his pictures framed and sent to his mother as a present.

He produced theorems rapidly, finishing at least one in a sitting. In February 5, 1833, he reported completing a large dish with a big watermelon and a knife sticking out of it in one evening of painting. In that same entry he noted he had purchased six yards of white velvet for 65 cents a yard.[2]

Although we have found one man who enjoyed painting theorems in the old days, it was usually women who did them. Some excellent pieces remain today, documented in some cases to women ancestors in certain families. These pieces are not faded by sun or light, and the white velvet has turned creamy, bringing warmth and richness to the colors. Such a theorem is the one we found in the print department at The Metropolitan Museum of Art in New York City. Packed away carefully with furniture stencils, it looks as new and vibrant as the day it was painted. (See fig. 122.) It was painted by Collata Holcomb of Granby, Connecticut. She was born in 1807 and died in 1887. She was twenty-five years younger than her husband Allen Holcomb, who was a furniture stenciler in Granby.

Most theorems were similar in size to Mrs. Holcomb's, which measures 10¾ x 13½", but a few were more elaborate. The example illustrated in figure 125 measures 27½" x 43½" and probably was created to cover the top of a dresser or table, judging by the rounded corners on the bottom edge. This theorem is a marvelous piece and is in truly extraordinary condition for its age.

In making a theorem, the artist applied rather dry paint to the velvet through the openings in the stencils, which were often called "theorems" themselves. The artist used small stiff brushes, sometimes called "scrubs." When she had blocked out the entire picture with her series of stencils, she added details freehand with a fine brush or a pen.[3] The artist usually cut her own stencils, but for a short period just before theorems went out of fashion about 1840, professionals cut them and sold them to theorem painters.

In those times it was probably considered not proper for ladies to stencil walls, but creating a theorem still life was very genteel. The word theorem may have come into use to distinguish the stenciling done by ladies from that of the itinerant craftsmen.

In the pages that follow we illustrate two patterns from the Holcomb theorem together with shell patterns that you may find useful to decorate towels for a guest bath and matching curtains. Don't forget that fruit patterns are always attractive in a kitchen.

122. **Colors Still Glowing.** Collata Holcomb of Granby, Connecticut, who was born in 1807, painted this theorem. The colors are so vivid here—the blue in the grapes and plums, and the red in the strawberries—that the theorem may never have hung on a wall. 10¾″ x 13½″. (The Metropolitan Museum of Art; Gift of Elizabeth Peck Shiff, 1947)

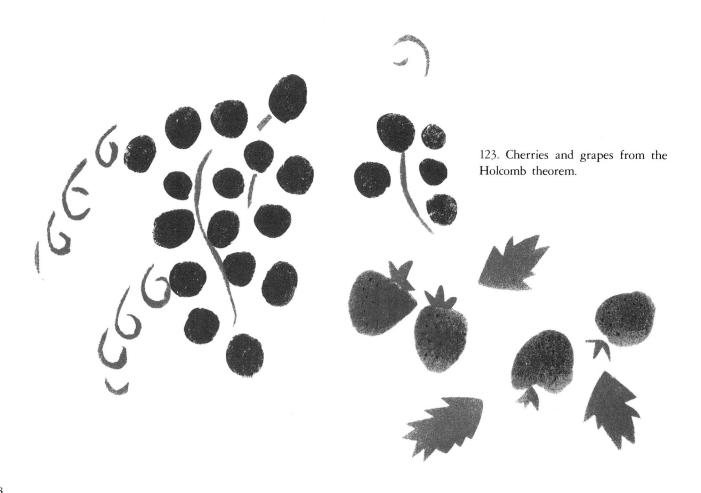

123. Cherries and grapes from the Holcomb theorem.

124. Seashell designs from a notebook.

125. **Extraordinary Theorem.** An unknown artist painted this elaborate theorem, which, judging from the rounded corners at the bottom, was intended to cover a dressing table or a chest of drawers. 27½″ x 43½″. (The Metropolitan Museum of Art; Anonymous Gift, 1949)

Chapter Nine

STEP-BY-STEP DIRECTIONS ON HOW TO STENCIL, TOGETHER WITH PATTERNS FROM AN EARLY AMERICAN CURTAIN, A VALANCE, AND A TABLECLOTH

We will be coaching you in this chapter, and this is what you will be prepared to do by the end of it:

▶ Stencil fabric: curtains, pillows, dust ruffles, placemats, terry towels, T-shirts, and more.

▶ Plan and stencil a quilt or coverlet.

▶ Make and stencil a tablecloth: tea, bridge, luncheon, or dinner size, with napkins to match.

▶ Stencil vinyl placemats, also vinyl shower curtains.

▶ Stencil tin, furniture, mailboxes, and other hard surfaces.

▶ Stencil floorcloths, window shades, and wallpaper.

▶ *And* we will give you handy tips that we have learned by trial and error over the years.

Your mind is bursting with ideas for using patterns from this book in your home and you are wondering just how difficult stenciling is. Why not try a simple project: stenciling placemats for your picnic table? Either quilted or vinyl mats are very inexpensive, and you will be so pleased with the results that you will want to stencil a set of cloth napkins with the same designs. As a result, you will have bright colorful place settings for your picnic table, and the experience with which to tackle a larger project.

Stenciling is simple: Cut the patterns out of clear vinyl or similar material, hold the stencils against the object to be decorated, and pounce paint through the holes.

It's easy and fun, and we are confident that our directions keep it that way for you.

I. HOW TO STENCIL
A. Materials

1. FOR STENCILS: Stencilers in the early 1800s used heavy paper that they oiled on both sides to keep the paint from bleeding through. What a mess! Today we use clear vinyls, mylars, and acetates instead. They are easier to cut and, more important, are *transparent,* which makes it a snap to line up one stencil over another. Vinyl plastic is sold at fabric and variety stores; mylar is sold at most drafting-supply houses. These products come in gauges: the higher the gauge, the thicker the material. Higher gauges are a bit more difficult to cut than the lower gauges, but they are more durable. For mylar use a gauge of .05 mill; for vinyl, a 12 gauge is suitable for most projects.

There is a heavy waxed paper, sold by the sheet in hobby stores, that also makes good stencils. (The kitchen variety will work in a pinch a very few times.)

2. CUTTING TOOLS: At a craft or hobby shop, buy a small, sharp knife that has a slim handle that allows you to cut as you hold it like a pencil. Try a curved or straight blade. Patty and Alice prefer a curved blade for cutting vinyl. Some prefer to use small straight-edge sewing scissors. A leather punch is ideal for cutting small circles.

3. BRUSHES: Buy several stencil brushes at a craft or hobby shop. They are fat and round with stubby black bristles and short handles. Tape them with masking tape about ½″ from the end of the bristles, to prevent the bristles from spreading and sneaking under the stencil. You can also use a round sash brush, sold in paint stores, but you must wrap it with masking tape so only about ¾″ of the bristles show. It helps to have one brush for each color, so buy several.

Some people stencil with a sponge, either synthetic or natural. Others prefer to stencil with a piece of toweling, cotton velvet, or wool wrapped around a forefinger.

Some prefer to use a fabric-stencil brush, which has white bristles that are longer than the black-bristle stencil brush. This brush is designed particularly for the swirling technique, which we will explain later. Do not wrap this brush with masking tape.

126. **Bedroom with a Country Flavor.** Stenciled walls, pillows, and other objects give this room a warm and homey feeling. Patricia Schad bought a plain quilted spread and stenciled it with the flowery vine. This is her bedroom in Huntingdon Valley, Pennsylvania; photograph by William Holland.

PAINT CHART

FOR FABRIC	FOR WALLS	FOR WOOD/TIN	FOR PAPER
fabric-stencil paint or dyes (the best to use)	latex wall paints (the best to use)	acrylic tube paints (the best to use)	all paints
silk screen paints	acrylic jar paints	latex paints	
acrylic tube paints with *matte medium* (2 parts paint to 1 part *medium*)		(on wood, protect the finished design with varnish for greater durability)	
acrylic jar paints			

4. PAINTS: For fabric, you can now buy water-soluble paints manufactured specifically for stenciling. Art, craft, and fabric shops carry them. Fabric paints are the type to use if you are stenciling material that will be washed many times.

If you are stenciling fabric that will receive light use, you can use either latex paint left over from painting your living room or artists' acrylic paints. You must mix artists' acrylic paints with a *matte medium* to extend the paint down into the fibers. Matte medium is sold in art stores and is a thick white substance that resembles glue. It does *not* dilute the color. Use two parts paint to one part matte medium.

For stenciling wood or tin, use acrylic tube paints from an art store or latex wall paint from a hardware or paint store; you must protect your completed design with a coat of varnish.

For stenciling paper, you can use latex wall paint, acrylic paints, or even fabric paints.

For stenciling walls, use latex wall paints, which come in a rich variety of colors.

5. MISCELLANEOUS ITEMS THAT ARE NEEDED:

a. Permanent markers with narrow tips for tracing patterns on your stencils.

b. A cutting surface such as a piece of glass, vinyl floor tile, or a cutting board sold specifically for cutting stencils. You can also use cardboard, magazines, or newspapers, but these will dull your knife.

c. Masking or drafting tape, which sticks less than masking tape.

d. A palette for your paints. You can start with a plastic plate, or styrofoam tray from under meats and fruits from the supermarket. You may want to move up to using an artist's gray palette, which will show color at its purest intensity.

e. Practice paper.

f. Old newspaper, rags, paper towels, and warm soapy water with which to clean up, plus a scouring pad to clean your stencils.

B. Cut Your Stencils

1. SELECT A PATTERN and cut a piece of vinyl (or whatever you are using as a stencil board) the size of the pattern plus a one-inch border all around—one piece for each color in the pattern. With a permanent marker trace the complete pattern on all pieces of the vinyl. Write "Top" on the front top of the stencils and an identification such as "bird, Janet Waring Collection." This is helpful when storing the pattern and locating it again.

2. CUT OUT YOUR STENCILS, one color on each piece of vinyl. For example, if red is the predominant color, cut the red area out of the first stencil and write "Red—stencil-1" on top.

3. CUT IN SWEEPING POSITIVE STROKES. Cut from the outside of the pattern towards the center. Punch out the inside pieces as you proceed. If your blade slips and you make too large a cut, simply mend the accidental cut with vinyl plastic tape.

C. Stenciling

1. COVER YOUR WORK SURFACE WITH PAPER and lay out your materials.

2. USE VERY LITTLE PAINT. Use a spoon and put one teaspoon of paint on your palette. Swirl the paint with your brush, using the *end* of the bristles, not the side as in fine arts painting. Now pound off any excess paint onto newspaper, paper toweling, or scrap paper.

Beginners usually use too much paint. Heavy, dark stenciling is not your object; you want light, soft, powdery stenciling as shown in this book. If your pounding results in a soft and powdery effect on the paper toweling or scrap paper, you are ready to stencil.

3. STENCIL THE PREDOMINANT COLOR FIRST. Pounce the paint of the predominant color through the stencil onto the paper. Hold your brush like a potato masher. Don't lift the stencil until you are finished covering the open areas. When you run out

127. Stencil A   + Stencil B   = Stencil AB

of paint, redip your brush and pounce off the excess on newspaper each time before continuing to stencil.

4. POUNCE OR SWIRL. Patty prefers to pounce the paint up and down; Alice also swirls. She says one should hold the brush perpendicular to the surface and gently swirl the brush clockwise over the stencil opening. Once you have covered it lightly with paint, repeat the process going counterclockwise. This method works well on fabric, pushing the paint gently into the fibers. Be careful not to use too much paint, as it will build up a heavy line along the edge of the stencil. All the patterns in this book were done with the pounce method except two groups—figures 50 through 58 from the Henry Ford Museum and Strawbery Banke.

5. BEGINNERS OFTEN TRY to control the amount of paint by pounding lightly. *Don't do this!* Your pounding stroke should be constant and even. Control the amount of paint by getting rid of the excess on newspaper.

6. WHEN YOU HAVE FINISHED THE FIRST COLOR, carefully lift your stencil and look at your work. If you had trouble getting the stencil up without smearing the design, you used too much paint. If tiny beads of paint appear on the underside of the stencil, you used too much paint. Wipe off both sides completely

and practice again until you get a design with the soft powdery look similar to the patterns in this book.

7. THIN COATS OF PAINT FROM STENCILING DRY QUICKLY. Allow a minute and then apply your second or third colors. Now you will see the design come to life. *(Remember to use a different brush or sponge for each color!)*

8. NOW THAT PRACTICE HAS MADE PERFECT, YOU ARE READY FOR A PROJECT, but first here's some necessary information.

a. *Cleaning up:* To clean your stencils, put them in a sink and rub them gently with hot water and a scouring pad to remove the paint. If the paint has hardened, soak the stencil in hot water and a detergent or rubbing alcohol for several hours or overnight.

Also wash your brushes or sponges, and dry thoroughly before using again. If you use a damp brush or sponge it will dilute your paint and result in messy stenciling. Use your hair dryer on the bristles if you're in a hurry.

b. *Storing your stencils:* Store the stencils flat in a file folder or manila envelope. Write the identification on the folder. This becomes more important as your collection of stencils grows, which it will.

Stenciling a Shaded Rose

Stenciling a delicate rose with many petals may look complicated, but it isn't. Here is how to create the flowers seen in the quilt belonging to the Museum of American Folk Art in figures 30 and 33.

First stencil lightly along the outer edges of the flower you plan to create. See Step A at the top of the opposite page. Then slide the stencil down and do a row of petals by stenciling only along the outer edge of the stencil, keeping your brush mostly on the stencil itself. See Step B. Be careful not to stencil outside the flower.

Continue until the rose is full of petals. See Step C.

| Step A | Step B | Step C |

II. STENCILING FABRIC

A. What fabrics can you use? You can stencil almost all fabrics: cottons, cotton blends, canvas, velvet, silk, velour, and prequilted materials. You can stencil terry cloth if you work the paint down into the fabric. *Avoid* knits, nylon, dacron, and other 100% synthetic fibers.

B. Prepare your fabric. No matter what material you choose, even ready-made curtains and sheets, wash it first to remove the sizing. Manufacturers treat all fabrics with sizing to stiffen them, and if the sizing is not washed out with soap and water, the stenciling will not adhere properly. Remove all wrinkles by ironing your material. Do not use a fabric softener.

The one exception to this rule is if you are stenciling a wall hanging that will never be laundered. Then you have no need to wash the fabric before stenciling.

C. Lay out your project. Cover your work surface with newspaper and a layer of paper toweling. If you are stenciling a T-shirt, put several layers of paper inside the shirt to absorb any excess paint and prevent it from bleeding through onto the back. If you use paper toweling for this, make sure it has a smooth surface; most paper toweling is textured and will give a corrugated or wavy look to your stenciling.

Tack your fabric as tautly as possible or tape it with masking tape. Mark guidelines for your designs with tailor's chalk or faint pencil lines.

D. Stencil away! See the previous stenciling instructions. If you are stenciling terry towels, you must work the paint down between the nap of the towels.

E. Set your designs with heat. The simplest method is to toss the fabric into a dryer at the *high* temperature setting for twenty to thirty minutes. You can also heat-set it by *dry ironing*, not steam ironing, for steam might well cause the stencil paint to run. Place a cloth over the designs and press for three to five minutes at the highest setting the fabric can tolerate without scorching. Or you can use your hairdryer and blow-dry the designs for three minutes. Check label for manufacturer's directions.

F. Care of stenciled fabrics. Machine wash; do not dry clean. Use the cool or cold-water, gentle cycle on your machine.

Shading

1. *To shade a flower*: Use a very dry brush and pound along the very outside edge of the stencil, your brush mostly on the stencil itself. You will find that a light amount of paint will shade towards the center of the flower. See the examples in figure 37.
2. *To shade gold*: This will tell you how to shade gold paint as seen in the peaches and plums in figure 76. First stencil the design in metallic acrylic gold. You can add a bit of acrylic bronze, or burnt umber, or red oxide to change the color to "old gold" but keep the metallic look. Then using a very dry brush, go over the gold with a color such as red or purple along one edge of the design. This will give that dimensional effect of shading.

III. STENCILING A QUILT, COVERLET, OR COUNTERPANE

A. With your new stenciling talents you can make a fine quilt, or a coverlet, which is a light summer spread, or a counterpane, which is a bedspread. A coverlet, once stenciled, simply has to be hemmed to be finished. This is also true for a counterpane, if you don't want to add fringe or a ruffle. Because of the stenciled designs, your piece may not need these additions; it will glow with color and pattern.

The dimensions for a commercial comforter in a twin size are 68" x 86"; full size is 76" x 86"; queen size is 86" x 86"; and king size is 102" x 90" or 86".

B. Consider the overall design. First, plot the design on paper, next, stencil the patterns on the paper, then arrange the stenciled patterns on an old sheet the size of your quilt.

If you want to avoid stenciling a large piece of material, you can work on quilt squares measuring 14", 16", or 18" square. Stencil the square and then sew them together. *Remember to allow a quarter inch extra all around for the seam allowance.*

C. Once you have stenciled your fabric, which you plan to

make into a quilt, find a good book on quilting and select your quilt-stitching design. A quilt shop is a good resource for help and information. You may prefer to stitch only around the stenciling or stitch diagonal lines up to the stenciling.

Stenciling Denim or any Dark Fabric

Most colors you stencil with will be lost on any dark-colored material. To compensate for this first stencil a light coat of white paint to block out that dark color. Then stencil over the white with any color you wish.

Often you'll get a slight ghost effect or "halo" around the edges from the white paint if you did not line up your second stenciling exactly over the white design. Don't give up; we think that the white halo effect is attractive.

128. Example of the halo effect.

IV. STENCILING A TABLECLOTH—TEA, BRIDGE, LUNCHEON, OR DINNER SIZE

You can buy a ready-made tablecloth and matching napkins on sale and use them for a new look on your table by stenciling them with patterns from this book. (Those inexpensive quilted placemats also stencil well.)

If you are making your cloth and napkins, here are the commercial dimensions:
Tea or bridge cloth: 52" square
Luncheon cloth: 52" x 70" (for four people)
Dinner cloth: 60" x 83" (for six people)
Dinner cloth: 60" x 102" (for eight people)
Napkins(tea or bridge): 14" square
Napkins (luncheon): 16"–19" square
Napkins(dinner): 20"–26" square

Can You Stencil Windowshades?

Yes. Do a stenciled border on the bottoms of your window shades, picking up colors in the room. It will give finishing touches to an area that is hard to curtain. When stenciling the shades, stencil several extremely thin layers of paint, allowing time for drying between applications. Paint that has been put on too thickly will crack when the shades are rolled up.

129. **Stenciled Window Shade.** Stenciling on sun-porch window shades and window frames gives a finished look to an area too large to curtain. Stenciled by Nancy Moormann; photograph by Barbara Marhoefer.

V. STENCILING VINYL PLACEMATS AND OTHER VINYL OBJECTS

A. Use new vinyl placemats. Clean off the surfaces. Cut your stencils and prepare the paints as above. If your design is to be in the center, determine the center of each mat and pencil in a faint dot. Place your first stencil on the mat and mark the dot on the stencil with a permanent marker; this is a register mark and all four, six, or eight mats will then be stenciled alike.

B. Paints. Use artists' acrylic paint straight from the tubes. *You do not need a matte medium.* Use stencil brushes, sponges, velvet, or wool.

C. Stenciling. Stencil the entire design in white lightly to block out the color of the mats. (Some dark colors do not cover well.) Stencil the white in almost a transparent effect, so you can still see the mat through the white. Now apply a very thin coat of the main colors over the white. Use several thin coats so the paint will not crack and peel. Often your stenciling will not be perfectly overlapped and you will see a white '"halo" after applying your

134

color. Let dry, move your stencil to cover the halo and stencil color over it. Or leave the halo to highlight your design.

D. If you make a mistake. The whole stencil can be removed with a wet rag within a few minutes of application.

E. To make it permanent. Spray the design with a quick-dry polyvarnish.

F. How to care for your mats. Clean with a sponge and liquid soap.

Stencil a Dust Ruffle

You have decided to create an American Country look in a bedroom that already has a plain bedspread and a one-color rug. Why not stencil a dust ruffle, picking up colors from both?

You don't even have to gather the ruffle if you use a scallop pattern similar to the one in figure 130. This Early American dust ruffle is just over 7′ long and 20″ deep—just enough to tuck under a mattress.

To make a pattern similar to the one on the ruffle use the leaves on the Janet Waring blanket chest (see fig. 94) and flowers as in figure 134, or the grapes in figure 117.

130. **Roses and Green Leaves.** Dust ruffle, maker unknown, c. 1835, Chepachet, New York. 89″ x 20″. The maker of this dust ruffle stenciled a scalloped pattern on linen cut to the length of one side of the bed. The piece is from the Mills-Harger family of Chepachet, located in Herkimer County, central New York State. (New York State Historical Association, Cooperstown, New York)

VI. STENCILING FURNITURE, MAILBOXES, TIN, AND OTHER HARD SURFACES

A. The method for stenciling fabric works here except you use even *less* paint on these hard surfaces. Try the effect of applying two thin coats of paint or one color over another color for a shaded effect.

B. For the gold stencils, as pictured in figures 76 and 85, apply a thin coat of metallic acrylic paint—silver, bronze, or gold; when dry, mix the metallic paint with a color, such as red, green, purple, or whatever. Then reapply the metallic color to highlight and shade individual elements in the design.

C. If you want a contemporary look on furniture, stencil in bright, clear colors and protect your work with flat or semigloss polyurethane varnish.

D. For an antique look, coat your work with an antiquing finish or with varnish (with raw umber added). Be sure to use oil-base color here for greatest durability.

E. If your stenciled object will be exposed to the weather, such as a mailbox, coat the finished piece with a quick-drying poly-spray varnish or marine varnish. Check with your paint store.

Can You Stencil Wallpaper?

You can stencil any wallpaper—plain paper, paper with vinyl coating, and 100% vinyl wall covering. You will get the best effect by stenciling on plain light-colored paper. If you are planning to stencil paper with a texture, test the patterns on a hidden spot to see how the texture affects the designs. You can also stencil stucco walls, plain plaster, and textured wallpaper.

VII. STENCILING A FLOORCLOTH

A. Early American folk wanted coverings for their stark wood floors, and as Oriental rugs were imported and very expensive, they settled for an inexpensive alternative made of canvas—stenciled floorcloths.

A floorcloth would be effective as a small rug for an entry way, in front of your hearth, under the pet dishes or in front of the kitchen sink. The last should be at least 2′ x 3′, a good size to work with. Later you might want to make a larger floorcloth to go under a table and some chairs.

B. For a small project, buy canvas in an art store that has been double primed—that is, canvas that has been painted with a primer on both sides and is ready for you to paint. This is good canvas to work with because the edges of the canvas do not fray; in fact, you cannot pull even one thread loose, so you will not have to hem it or glue under the edges to prevent unraveling. It is ideal for a narrow hall runner or even placemats for a picnic table.

C. When you want to make a floorcloth that is wider than the double-primed canvas, go to a tent and awning manufacturer. You must then prime it yourself.

1. Buy No. 10 weight canvas, which comes 36″ to 72″ wide. Try not to wrinkle the canvas on your way home because large wrinkles are almost impossible to iron out with a household iron. Ask the store clerk to put your canvas on an empty cardboard spool if possible.

2. Spread brown wrapping paper out on your basement floor and lay the canvas down. Cover it with gesso or latex primer on both sides. Gesso is a heavy paint available in art stores used to prime artists' canvas. Paint one or two coats of basepaint over the top, using any latex paint you wish for a background color.

3. When the paint is dry, measure on the back the exact size you wish your floorcloth to be so that you have pencil lines to

131. **Summer Placemat.** Brighten your picnic table with a set of placemats like this watermelon slice. It is made of canvas like floorcloth, then painted and stenciled. See our easy directions for making a floorcloth. Photograph by Alice Fjelstul.

help with the hemming. Add 3/4″ to 1″ around the edges for turning under.

4. Miter the corners, so that the excess bulk is eliminated when you glue them down. Then glue down the edges, using white household glue, tacky craft glue or, best of all, a white fabric-and-leather cement used to repair canvas.

D. Now you are ready to stencil. Make paper mockups of your patterns and arrange them on the canvas until you are satisfied with your overall plan.

E. With a hard-lead pencil draw a light dotted line through the center of the floorcloth vertically and another horizontally.

F. If you are planning to use a vine on the border, you might want to stencil a flower in each corner. Then you do not have to worry about how to bend around the corners. The border should be 1″ from the edge.

G. To finish the floorcloth, apply three coats of varnish. The first coat should be thinned according to the formula of two parts varnish to one part thinner. Polyurethane varnish tends to yellow so do not use it on light background colors such as white. Use a non-yellowing varnish instead.

H. Your floorcloth may develop hairline cracks. Do not worry. All the floorcloths in museums have cracks. They in no way effect the serviceability of the floorcloth and give it an antique patina.

I. You don't need a pad under your floorcloth. Put it directly on a wood floor or even on ceramic tile. To prevent slipping and skidding, spray it lightly with an antiskid rug-backing spray.

J. To clean your floorcloth, wash it with a damp mop and a good cleaner, while you are washing your kitchen floor.

VIII. HANDY TIPS

A. *Our Early American Fudge Factor.* In our study of wall stenciling we noticed that Early American itinerant stencilers improvised at the corners of rooms and over doorways. They often used an extra element of the design or changed the spacing as they turned the corner. They were not hampered by precise measuring and neither should you be, more than a hundred years later!

B. To achieve an antique look to any color, add a bit of raw umber. You'll be surprised when you see how it adds seventy-five years to your stenciling.

C. Finish furniture with an antique glaze, usually with an oil base, to add a protective finish as well as an antique look. You can buy it at a paint or hardware store.

D. Experiment and discover the effects of using acrylic silver, bronze, and gold paints mixed in with your other colors.

E. Use vodka(!) to remove dried acrylic or latex paint when it accidentally gets where it is unwanted.

132. **Unpainted Chest, Canvas Floor Cloth.** This is an inexpensive unpainted chest of drawers that has been stenciled in the American country manner. Artist canvas was used for the floorcloth. Directions for making a floorcloth are given in this chapter, along with directions on how to stencil—so easy that it can be mastered by *anyone*!

Patterns from an Early American Curtain, Valance, and Tablecloth

Here are photographs and patterns from a window curtain, valance, and a tablecloth, all dating from Early American times. They are illustrated in the original colors.

133. Valance with Vandyking. Stenciled valance, maker unknown, from the home of Samuel and Lydia Jenness, c. 1830, Lowell, Massachusetts. 14⅜″ high. This charming valance has a border of blue triangles, an example of vandyking, which is easy to do and gives a nice finish. Vandyking is named for the Flemish painter Anthony Van Dyck (1599–1641), and it can take the form of triangles, points, or scallops suggested by the wide collars of linen and lace with scalloped or pointed edges, which were an important part of the rich clothing worn by the subjects in his portraits. (Old Sturbridge Village; photograph by Henry E. Peach)

134. Try It. To make a vandyked border, cut a stencil with a series of four triangles; then stencil along the edge of your fabric, move the stencil and repeat the process.

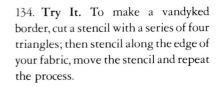

135. **Roses at the Window.** Window curtain (one of a pair). Maker unknown, 1825–1840, New England. 32″ x 16″. How these colorful rose-covered curtains must have brightened a window with a drab winter landscape outside! Notice the extra rose in the lower left corner; it probably hung at the center of the window. (Old Sturbridge Village; photograph by Henry E. Peach)

136. Pattern from the curtain.

137. **Cornucopia of Flowers.** Tablecloth, factory woven cotton, maker unknown, c. 1840, New England. 25″ x 29″. The maker of this tablecloth stenciled it elegantly with a border of roses and a large cornucopia of roses and spring flowers in the center. We present the cornucopia here, reduced in size. (Old Sturbridge Village; photograph by Henry E. Peach)

138. Cornucopia stencil.

NOTES

Chapter One

1. Janet Waring, *Early American Stencils on Walls and Furniture* (1937; reprint ed., New York: Dover Publications, 1968), p. 87.
2. *Ibid.*
3. *Ibid.*, p. 133.
4. *Ibid.*, p. 87.
5. Holger Cahill, *American Folk Art: The Art of the Common Man in America 1750-1900.* (New York: W.W. Norton for The Museum of Modern Art, 1932), p. 3.
6. Jean Lipman and Alice Winchester, *The Flowering of American Folk Art 1776-1876* (New York: The Viking Press in Cooperation with the Whitney Museum of American Art, 1974), p. 6.
7. William R. Scott of William R. Scott, Inc., publishers, telephone interview, March 10, 1980.
8. Marjorie W. von Suck, "The Janet Waring Collection of Stencils," *Old-Time New England* (Bulletin of The Society for the Preservation of New England Antiquities) 44, no. 4 (Spring 1954), pp. 100–102.
9. Cyril I. Nelson & Carter Houck, *The Quilt Engagement Calendar Treasury* (New York, E.P. Dutton, Inc., 1982), p. 176.

Chapter Two

1. Florence Peto, *American Quilts and Coverlets* (New York: Chanticleer Press, 1949), p. 19.
2. *Ibid.*
3. Patsy and Myron Orlofsky, *Quilts in America* (New York: McGraw-Hill Book Company, 1974), p. 11.
4. *Ibid.*, p. 153.
5. *Ibid.*, p. 152.
6. Rose Wilder Lane, *Woman's Day Book of American Needlework* (New York: Simon & Schuster, 1963), p. 57.
7. Beth Gutcheon, *The Perfect Patchwork Primer* (New York: David McKay, 1973), p. 12.
8. Patsy and Myron Orlofsky, *Quilts in America*, p. 141.
9. Peto, *American Quilts and Coverlets*, p. 22.
10. *Ibid.*, p. 19.
11. Orlofsky, *Quilts in America*, p. 177.

Chapter Four

1. Shirley Spaulding DeVoe, *The Tinsmiths of Connecticut* (Middletown, Conn.: Wesleyan University Press, 1968), p. 30.
2. *Ibid.*, p. 97; also correspondence with author, November 16, 1982.
3. *Ibid.*, p. 134
4. Mariette Paine Slayton, *Early American Decorating Techniques* (New York: The Macmillan Company, 1972), p. 3
5. DeVoe, *Tinsmiths*, p. 3.
6. Slayton, *Decorating Techniques*, p. 3
7. DeVoe, *Tinsmiths*, p. 158.
8. *Ibid.*, p. 11.
9. *Ibid.*, p. 32.
10. Shirley Spaulding DeVoe, "Women Industrial Painters of Connecticut, 1779–1880," *The Decorator* (Journal of the Historical Society of Early American Decoration) 37, no. 1 (Fall 1982), p. 12; also DeVoe, *Tinsmiths*, p. 34.
11. Violet Milnes Scott, "The Influence of Esther Stevens Brazer on the Decorative Arts," in W. D. John and Jacqueline Simcox, *English Decorated Trays* (Newport, England: The Ceramic Book Company, 1964), p. 187.
12. Esther Stevens Brazer, *Early American Decoration*, (Springfield, Mass.: The Pond-Ekberg Co., 1940), p. ix.
13. Scott, "Influence of Esther Stevens Brazer," p. 187.
14. Shirley Spaulding DeVoe, *The Art of the Tinsmith, English and American* (Exton, Pa.: Schiffer Publishing, 1981), p. 150.
15. Mrs. Robert Keegan, interview, March 14, 1983.
16. Brazer, *Early American Decoration*, p. ix.
17. Scott, "Influence of Esther Stevens Brazer," p. 188.

Chapter Five

1. William R. Scott of William R. Scott, Inc., publishers, correspondence, October 26, 1981.
2. Waring, *Early American Stencils*, p. 87.
3. This quote is from an unidentified, undated newspaper clipping taped inside the top of the blanket chest stenciled by Janet Waring and formerly owned by her greatniece Barbara Hunt Smith. The clipping reported that the chest had been displayed at the Architectural League.
4. Waring, *Early American Stencils*, p. 87.
5. *Ibid.*, p. 112.
6. *Ibid.*, p. 116.
7. *The Magazine Antiques* (December 1937), p. 325.
8. Francis W. Reader, "Further Notes on the Use of the Stencil in Mural Decoration," *The Archaeological Journal* (publication of the Royal Archaeological Society of Great Britain and Ireland) 97 (1940), pp. 90–94.
9. *Ibid.*
10. James Ayres, *British Folk Art* (Woodstock, N.Y.: The Overlook Press, 1977), p. 107.
11. William R. Scott, correspondence, October 26, 1981.
12. Barbara Hunt Smith, interview, February 21, 1980.
13. Von Suck, "Janet Waring Collection," p. 100.
14. Waring, *Early American Stencils*, p. 88.
15. *Ibid.*
16. *Ibid.*, p. ix.

17. We have tried for five years to find a photograph or picture of Miss Waring, and have had no success.

Chapter Six

1. James Thomas Flexner, *Washington: The Indispensable Man* (Boston and Toronto: Little Brown, 1969), p. 4.

Chapter Eight

1. "Another Note on Theorem Painting," *The Magazine Antiques* 21, no. 6 (June 1932), pp. 258–259.
2. *Ibid.*
3. Waring, *Early American Stencils*, p. 137.

BIBLIOGRAPHY

AYRES, JAMES. *British Folk Art.* Woodstock, N.Y.: The Overlook Press, 1977.

BISHOP, ROBERT. *New Discoveries in American Quilts.* New York: E.P. Dutton & Company, Inc., 1975.

BRAZER, ESTHER STEVENS. *Early American Decoration.* Springfield, Mass.: The Pond-Ekberg Co., 1940. Third printing 1950.

CAHILL, HOLGER. *American Folk Art: The Art of the Common Man in America 1750-1900.* New York: W.W. Norton for the Museum of Modern Art, 1932.

CHURCH, DIANA. "The Bayless Stenciled Quilt." *Uncoverings, 1983.* Seminar, Mill Valley, California, October 21–23, 1983.

DEVOE, SHIRLEY SPAULDING. *The Art of the Tinsmith, English and American.* Exton, Pa.: Schiffer Publishing, 1981.

————. *The Tinsmiths of Connecticut.* Middletown, Conn.: Wesleyan University Press, 1968.

————. "Women Industrial Painters of Connecticut, 1779–1880." *The Decorator* (Journal of the Historical Society of Early American Decoration) 37, no. 1 (Fall 1982).

DUNTON, WILLIAM RUSH, JR., M.D. *Old Quilts.* Catonsville, Md.: published by the author at 33 North Symington Avenue, 1946.

FALES, DEAN A., JR. *American Painted Furniture 1660-1880.* New York: E.P. Dutton, 1972.

FJELSTUL, ALICE BANCROFT, and SCHAD, PATRICIA BROWN, with MARHOEFER BARBARA. *Early American Wall Stencils in Color.* New York: E.P. Dutton, 1982.

FLEXNER JAMES THOMAS. *Washington: The Indispensable Man.* Boston and Toronto: Little, Brown, 1969.

GUTCHEON, BETH. *The Perfect Patchwork Primer.* New York: David McKay, 1973.

HUTCHINGS, DOROTHY DEAN. *A Quarter Century of Decorating and Teaching Country Painting.* Tucson, Ariz.: published by the author at 1509 W. Delano Drive, 1975.

JOHN, W. D., and SIMCOX, JACQUELINE. *English Decorated Trays.* Newport, England: The Ceramic Book Company, 1964.

KENNEY, JOHN TARRANT. *The Hitchcock Chair.* New York: Clarkson N. Potter, 1971.

LANE, ROSE WILDER. *Woman's Day Book of American Needlework.* New York: Simon & Schuster, 1963.

NELSON, CYRIL I. & HOUCK, CARTER. *The Quilt Engagement Calendar Treasury.* New York: E.P. Dutton, Inc., 1982.

ORLOFSKY, PATSY, and ORLOFSKY, MYRON. *Quilts in America.* New York: McGraw-Hill Book Company, 1974.

PETO, FLORENCE. *American Quilts and Coverlets.* New York: Chanticleer Press, 1949.

————. *Historic Quilts.* New York: The American Historical Co., 1939.

PETTIT, FLORENCE H. *America's Printed & Painted Fabrics.* New York: Hastings House, 1970.

READER, FRANCIS W. "Further Notes on the Use of the Stencil in Mural Decoration." *The Archaeological Journal* (publication of the Royal Archaeological Society of Great Britain and Ireland) 97 (1940).

————. "The Use of the Stencil in Mural Decoration." *The Archaeological Journal* (publication of the Royal Archaeological Society of Great Britain and Ireland) 95 (1938).

REINERT, GUY F. *Pennsylvania German Coverlets.* Kutztown, Pa.: published by Mrs. C. Naaman Keyser for Pennsylvania German Folklore Society, 1949.

SAFFORD, CARLETON L., and BISHOP, ROBERT. *America's Quilts and Coverlets.* New York: Weathervane Books, 1960.

SLAYTON, MARIETTE PAINE. *Early American Decorating Techniques.* New York: The Macmillan Company, 1972.

VON SUCK, MARJORIE W. "The Janet Waring Collection of Stencils." *Old-Time New England* (The Bulletin of The Society for the Preservation of New England Antiquities) 44, no. 4 (Spring 1954).

WARING, JANET. *Early American Stencils on Walls and Furniture.* New York: William R. Scott, 1937. Reprint. New York: Dover Publications, 1968.

ALICE FJELSTUL is a native of Philadelphia, and graduated from Wheaton College, Norton, Massachusetts, with a major in the history of art. During the Bicentennial, Alice Fjelstul pursued her interest in Early American arts and crafts. Dressed in mobcaps and long skirts, she and Patricia Schad demonstrated stenciling at Colonial craft shows and went on to receive a grant from the National Endowment for the Arts to document original New England wall stenciling.

Today, transplanted to Plymouth, Minnesota, she continues her study of traditional arts and crafts and teaches folk art and stenciling at the Art Center of Minnesota and the Wayzata Quilting Emporium. She emphasizes the ease and fun of stenciling in the classes she gives throughout the country.

In addition to her teaching, Alice has a stenciling company that produces stencils and hand-stenciled decorative accessories. She claims the cold of Minnesota is conducive to spending long hours in the stencil process.

PATRICIA SCHAD's roots are in New England, so her research has been especially rewarding. She was born in Maine, is a graduate of Bucknell University with a bachelor of science degree in biochemistry, and has a master's degree in education from Boston University. She studied design at the Philadelphia College of Art.

Her research has led her all through New England and as a result, she has become an avid collector of stenciled pieces, many of them illustrated in this book.

Her other interests include travel, archaeology, golf, and platform tennis. She has done biochemical research, and taught science. Now she conducts stenciling workshops around the country. Patty has her own stenciling company and produces stencils and hand-stenciled decorative items.

She resides with her husband and three children in Huntingdon Valley, Pennsylvania.

BARBARA MARHOEFER has learned a great deal about stenciling and quilting since she began writing with Alice and Patty. Their first book was *Early American Walls Stencils in Color*, published in 1982 by E.P. Dutton. Barbara is a graduate of Trinity College, Washington, D.C., and the Columbia University Graduate School of Journalism. She was an instructor in the Journalism Department at Temple University for three years. She has worked for three newspapers, the latest being *The New York Times* on a part-time basis.

Her first book was *Witches, Whales, Petticoats and Sails, 300 Years of Adventures and Misadventures in Long Island History*. It is used to teach Long Island history in elementary schools on Long Island.